DOING BUSINESS WITH KOREANS

DOING BUSINESS WITH KOREANS

Published by Okdang Books, Inc.

#902 Samna Midas, 590-2 Sungsan-dong
Mapo-gu, Seoul 121-250, Republic of Korea
tel: 82-2-722-6826　fax:82-2-723-6486
www.okdangbooks.com
e-mail: coolsey@okdangbooks.com

ISBN 978-89-93952-42-1　03320
CIP 2012001686

Printed in Republic of Korea

First printing May 25, 2012

DOING BUSINESS WITH KOREANS

KNOWING KOREA
WILL GUARANTEE
BUSINESS SUCCESS

Prof. SEOIL CHAIY

Okdang Books

Introduction

In a globalized world, products, services, capital, labor, and ideas can move freely as a single, massive economy without geographical boundaries. Granted, the obstacles and constraints may vary based on region and country, but the trend toward corporate globalization is accelerating with the development of transportation, communication and eased regulations by countries around the world.

What must we overcome in order to facilitate global business? We must overcome cultural differences. Because each country's culture and history has contributed to the rise of unique values and customs, the reactions of culturally diverse people may differ from others within a given situation.

Language is without a doubt the most important component in communication. Moreover, recognizing and respecting others' culture is also very important. In order to understand the culture of a country, understanding its sub-elements is very helpful. While we can certainly reduce the language barrier by becoming multilingual or by using interpreters, if we fail to understand others' unique cultural characteristics, we are bound to have misunderstanding and conflict.

Cultural differences results dissimilarity in behavior that we cannot easily judge which is right or wrong as such dissimilarity originates from historical and cultural backgrounds. It is important for us to see that these dissimilarities are "different" because we are from different cultures, not "wrong." We need to put efforts in together to truly understand each other's differences and respect them because it is a two-way street, not one. Remember, it takes two to tango.

This book discusses the cultural characteristics of Korea and Koreans, and business environment within Korean organizations. I believe through this book you can understand the cultural differences between you and Korea, Koreans and Korean organizations to improve communications and productivity in a multinational business environment. I hope all the efforts you put in will lay a solid foundation to lead you to be ahead in global competition.

Seoil Chaiy

Professor of Business Administration,
School of Business,
Korea University

Contents

Chapter 01

Knowing Korea

We will learn about Korea's cultural characteristics to understand and recognize the differences between Asian and Western cultures. I believe that through this book, you will be able to communicate more efficiently within multinational organizations and, in turn, improve business efficiency.

You will learn the importance of global management and communications as well as general information about Korea and its people. After this chapter, you will have gained basic concepts of management and the importance of corporate communication in globalizing world. You will also gain basic knowledge on how to communicate with Koreans.

First, let us look at the conversation between a Korean and a Westerner.

skit

Westerner and Korean meet and shake hands.

Korean: Hello, nice to meet you. My name is Minsoo Kim.

Westerner: Hello, my name is Tom. Nice to meet you.

Korean: Tom, you look much younger than I expected.

Westerner: (surprised) Wow, thank you. Mr. Kim, I was told that you're a marketing manager at A Group.

Korean: Yes. Since I am in a lower position and also younger than you, you can be comfortable with me.

Westerner: Oh, no. That's not important to me. Well then, shall we sit down?

Westerner and Korean sitting at a restaurant.

Korean: By the way, where are you from?

Westerner: (To himself: Why is he asking me where I am from when we just met?) Well, I'm from Romania.

Korean: Oh, I visited there because I had business in Bucharest. By any change do you live near there?

Westerner: Oh, no. I live near Sibiu.

Korean: Oh, that's too bad!

Westerner: (To himself: Why does he think it's too bad?) Where are you from, Mr. Kim?

Korean: Oh, I'm from Korea.

Westerner: I see. Would you happen to be from North Korea?

Korean: (flustered) Oh, no. I am South Korean. Have you ever been to Korea before?

Westerner: (To himself: Why is he asking me all these questions when we are running out of time?) No, not yet. But, I think I might be going there next year.

Korean: Yes, please come! Places such as my hometown Jeju Island are so beautiful.

Westerner: Oh, a Romanian friend of mine visited there and told me what a beautiful island it is. I would definitely want to visit there when I go to Korea.

Korean: (very pleased) Oh! You know about Jeju Island! When you visit South Korea, I will personally show you around the island.

Westerner: (laughs with pleasure) That would be great!

Korean: You seem like a really great person, Tom. Since we are short on time, let's get started.

Westerner: Yes, sure!

What you just saw was a typical first conversation between a Korean and a Westerner. In today's globalized world, working with other nationals or ethnic groups has become very common. I enjoy travelling to other countries because I can observe and learn new things. At the same time, however, I feel strange by unfamiliarities when I interact with the local people and when I deal with different customs. Nevertheless, we are all humans; most of our day-to-day living isn't all that different. We share far more similarities than differences.

I'm sure that you've experienced this yourself but, travelling abroad or talking to foreigners may not always be easy. Especially when communicating with non-native English speakers, it can be difficult to understand exactly what the other person is trying to say. Sometimes, I feel puzzled when I say something and the other person reacts differently than I had anticipated due to cultural differences.

The cultural differences between Asian and Western cultures may seem particularly pronounced when people of these areas meet for the first time. Even the way they greet is different. Generally, Westerners shake hands when greeting one another or hug or put their cheeks together if they are close to one another. Asians greet by bowing to one another. If you hug an Asian on first acquaintance, he or she will probably be uncomfortable. Thus, when meeting a person from different ethnic background for the first time may be perplexing or awkward.

1

Globalizing and Globalization

The world is getting smaller every day. To what extent has globalization impacted our lives?

1 What Does "Globalization" Mean?

In a globalized world, products, services, capital, labor, and ideas can move freely within a single, massive economy without geographical boundaries. Granted, the obstacles and constraints may vary based on region and country, but the trend toward corporate globalization is accelerating with the development of transportation, communication and eased regulations around the world. Globalization is often referred to as being "worldwide." Of course, some define globalization and "worldwide" differently, but for our purposes, it will be sufficient to consider them as equivalent.

Since ancient times, people have traded necessary goods with neighboring countries. With the development of transportation, these trades expanded further to distant countries. This phenomenon progressed rapidly after the end of World War II. In order to adapt to local markets and increase price competitiveness with cheap local labor, corporations began forming joint venture companies with local partners or established and operated its own independent branches. These internationalization practices have become quite standard for today's international corporations. There are myriad other ways that corporations can internationalize — however since this is beyond the scope of this book, we will skip this discussion.

2 What Is Global Business?

How would you define "global business"? Global business refers to a company's business activities that involve two or more countries. It also refers to influences by various business environments such as global markets, regional markets, and national markets. Because corporations conduct businesses across borders, they must be able to read and manage the flow of the global economy and markets. However, because business is conducted by people who use different languages, communication problems inevitably occurs.

Here is an interesting story related to global business:

Did you know that there was a time when a grain of pepper was worth as much as a grain of gold? Medieval Europeans considered spices to be very precious. Among these, they considered pepper to be the most precious spice.

Why was pepper so valuable? Pepper was considered extremely valuable because it was transported from India to Europe via long trade routes. Pepper became a symbol of status due to its scarcity and value. As a result, possessing pepper, as well as other spices, symbolized high class, status, and power. Pepper was not only used in food, but served a monetary function as well. It was used as gifts, listed as part of inheritances, and often used as a means of payment instead of gold.

However, the powerful Ottoman Empire's conquest of Christian Constantinople in 1453 closed off the spice trade route between Europe and Asia over land and gave the seagoing merchants of Venice a monopoly on spices, particularly pepper, from India. Venetian merchants sold pepper 600 times the price of their initial purchase. As a result, other Europeans sought a reliable and less costly way to obtain spices by opening a new sea route to India along the coast of Africa and around the Cape of Good Hope. This is an early example of global business.

Now let us learn about trade dependence. A country's trade dependence is calculated by the amount of goods traded (the total of export and import goods) divided by the current domestic product (GDP, Gross Domestic Product). Trade dependence shows how much trading is conducted in a country. By looking at trade dependence, we can determine how much a country's economy depends on exports and imports. In Korea, as well as the Czech Republic, trade dependence is relatively high. In 2008, Korea's trade dependence was 92.3 percent, and the Czech Republic's was 133 percent. In contrast, dependence on trade was 41.2 percent in the United Kingdom.

In general, more populous and developed countries have low trade dependence, while in less populous countries where the domestic market is small or the export market is large, have high trade dependence.

3 Cultural Differences and Communication

What must we overcome in order to facilitate global business? We must overcome cultural differences. Because each country's culture and history has contributed to the rise of unique values and customs, the reactions of culturally diverse people may differ from a homogenous population in a given situation.

Let us take a closer look at when two people from different cultures meet for the first time.

Skit

A Korean and a Westerner greet each other upon meeting for the first time.

Korean: Hello.

Westerner: Hello. Nice to meet you.

Korean: My name is Minsoo Kim.

Westerner: I am Tom.

Korean: You're from the UK, right?

Westerner: Yes, I am from Edinburgh.

Korean: I'm from Seoul, South Korea's capital. I'm 32 years old. How old are you?

Westerner: (surprised and puzzled) . . . .

The Westerner meets another Westerner and begins to converse.

Westerner: That's what happened! Why would someone ask that to a stranger?

In Korea, it is common to ask the other person's age when meeting for the first time. This can make the other person uncomfortable if he or she is from another country. Similarly, it is possible that questions and responses that are commonly accepted in one country may be considered inappropriate in another country. Therefore, in a globalized business environment, it is important to facilitate communication by first trying to understand others' cultures.

Language is without a doubt the most important component in

communication. Moreover, recognizing and respecting others' culture is also very important. In order to understand the culture of a country, understanding its sub-elements is very helpful. While we can certainly reduce the language barrier by becoming multilingual or by using interpreters, if we fail to understand others' unique cultural characteristics, we are bound for misunderstanding and conflict.

You may have observed cultural differences from various companies, which may or may not be aligned with what is illustrated in this book. However, this book aims to explain the general corporate culture of Korean companies, therefore we will limit our discussion to national characteristics. We will proceed to look at cultural differences in communication and how effective communication can increase work productivity.

4 The Importance of Communication

It is not easy to work as a team with people from other countries. Striving for the same goal and performing at one's best can be difficult with differences in language and values. However, businesses cannot survive the global competition if they cannot work together as a team.

When people from multiple countries work together, the lack of cultural awareness may cause a stressful work environment. Miscommunication can stem from the language barriers and it can lead to mistrust and disruptions at work. These issues can be resolved rather quickly when working in the same location rather than in different places. I hope that this book will be the first step to resolve miscommunication problems.

2

Management and Communication

Communication within organizations is becoming increasingly important with globalization. Let us briefly review the concepts behind management and communication.

1 What Is Management?

First, let us consider what "management" is. Management is a commonly used term in modern society. Management began with corporations and is still typically used in reference to corporations, but this concept also applies to non-profit organizations as well. Management targets people-related issues.

Management unites people with different skills and knowledge toward a common goal, such as combining various functions like marketing, finance, production, sales, and R&D. In this process, the role of management is to enhance the benefits and compensate for the shortcomings of the workers.

Management integrates people and therefore is heavily embedded in culture. No matter where you are in the world, business executives will have the same tasks, but their methods may vary due to differences in cultural backgrounds.

The most important factor in management is for all members to share same values. As part of this process, companies must make an effort to educate workers and contribute to society as the company grows.

2 What Is Communication?

Communication is typically defined as the social process of an individual, group, or organization exchanging or sharing messages and information. Effective communication is critical for multinational companies. It is important that people of different cultures and languages strive to communicate accurately and mobilize towards a common goal in a timely manner while quickly adapting to changes. In general, for both multinational and local companies, communication is considered the most fundamental business activity.

Now let us consider an everyday situation where communication occurs between multinational workers. Consider the following skit and learn the communication differences between employees from different parts of the world.

Skit

Mr. Kim walking into the United Kingdom office.

Narrator: Mr. Kim has travelled from the Seoul office to the UK office this morning, where Mr. Smith is. Excluding his family vacation to Southeast Asia, Mr. Kim has never had business trips outside of Korea.

Mr. Kim walks uneasily as he thinks about how he will communicate in English.

Narrator: Mr. Kim's English is not fluent and he is also not accustomed to British accent. He has had English classes at school where he was taught American English but has never used English on daily basis. So, he is afraid to speak and attempt to understand spoken English.

Mr. Smith and Mr. Kim shake hands. Mr. Smith greets Mr. Kim and introduces himself.

Mr. Smith: You've come a long way. You must be tired, aren't you?

Mr. Kim: (smiles brightly) Oh, yes.

Narrator: Actually, Mr. Kim wanted to reply, "No, I'm not tired at all." However, since he is not fluent in English, he simply replied, "Yes." which actually meant "Yes, I feel tired."

Mr. Smith is a bit confused because Mr. Kim's facial expressions and tone of voice do not indicate that he was tired, yet he answered that he was "tired."

Koreans find it difficult to directly say "no." Because of this, negative questions can lead to communication confusion. We will look at this specific portion of communication in a later chapter.

3

First Meeting with Koreans

1 What Koreans Are Curious about

When Koreans meet someone for the first time, they are most interested in the other person's age, position/title, and where they are from. Those from Europe or other multi-cultural regions where people regularly encounter various ethnic groups may not be as concerned about where the other person is from. But for Koreans who come from a homogeneous country, consider it as a very important question.

Also, the other person's age and position/title are important information to Koreans because they value hierarchy. In Korea, hierarchy determines your manners with others.

When meeting a foreigner, Koreans are also very curious of the other person's ethnicity and nationality. You may be puzzled when a newly acquainted Korean asks you, "Where are you from?" or "Where is your hometown?" Koreans ask these questions with a subconscious tendency to stereotype the foreigner and find connections and similarities with themselves. A typical Korean would be very glad to hear that a foreigner knows someone in Korea or has previously been to Korea.

2 Thoughts of Koreans

Why do Koreans want to find a connecting link? Koreans have a tendency to identify themselves as a member of a group. Asians typically construct their identity based on their families, friends, and siblings. Therefore, Asians tend to become anxious when they feel isolated. This is in contrast to Westerners, for whom individuality plays a big part in constructing their identity.

In other words, Koreans (and this may apply to all Asians) define themselves in relation to the people they have a close relationship with. That is why they feel more comfortable when they find common ground with others; common ground is considered as having a connection with others.

3 First Meeting with Koreans

Do you remember the first skit in this chapter?

Much like Mr. Kim in the skit, one thing Koreans wonder about when meeting a foreigner is their hometown. Foreigners often find it hard to understand why Koreans ask such personal questions that are unrelated to work. However, you will find that if a foreigner is from a location where the Korean has been to, the Korean will be very happy to know that.

If a common link is not found, then Mr. Kim will make another attempt. For example, he might ask, "Have you been to Korea?" If common link is still not found, then he will probably continue to make another attempt at finding a common link. If you say that you have been to Korea, you will most likely receive follow up questions such as, "When did you go?" or "Where did you visit?" These questions will most likely stop when Mr. Kim finds something in common whether it's something both parties know about, places they've been to, or things they like, and Mr. Kim feels comfortable starting a relationship.

Moreover, Mr. Kim will be very sensitive to your position and age. This information is needed when establishing a relationship because it is essential for Mr. Kim to build mental hierarchy of the relationship, which he will then use for appropriate words and actions.

Also, Mr. Kim will show keen interest in how much you know about Korea. This is because when Mr. Kim first meets you, he sees himself and his country as one entity. From the moment he sets foot in a foreign country, he subconsciously believes that he represents

Korea. Thus, if you know a lot about Korea, then he comes to the conclusion that this is beneficial for him. Others may not identify themselves as one entity with their own country, but most Koreans share this feeling to some degree. Therefore, many would say that all Koreans become patriotic when they go abroad or meet foreigners.

If you were to ask Mr. Kim, "Where are you from?" when you first meet him, his answer will probably be "Korea." If you ask with a follow up question "North or South Korea?", he will feel offended and answer "South." Koreans are quite sensitive to this question partly because South Koreans think that they represent Korea. It is also because they do not want to accept North Korea as an independent nation. Nevertheless, foreigners naturally ask such question because they are unsure, not to offend the South Koreans.

Koreans can only converse comfortably about work after building a common ground and knowing where each party stands in the relationship. Westerners may find that the Koreans who ask such private questions extremely rude, or feel that it is a waste of time. However, knowing why Koreans ask such questions will help them understand this behavior. This subject will be covered in detail in a later chapter.

4

General Information about Korea

1 Thoughts about Korea

Griffis, who introduced Korea to the American West about 130 years ago, defined Korea as "The Hermit Nation." It has also been called the "Land of the Morning Calm" by Lowell. Korea was a quiet, rural country about 130 years ago, where even the cities resembled the countryside. It would have seemed relatively uncivilized in the eyes of Westerners.

Foreigners may associate Korea with terms like, "war, poverty, civil division, student riots or great economic success." Younger foreigners may associate Korea with the World Cup, K-Pop, Korean soap operas, and economic development.

2 The Status of Korea

South Korea's position in the global market is outstanding in many ways. Korea's semiconductor production rate is number one in the world and is the world leader in shipbuilding. Moreover, it is number one in steel manufacturing and has the highest broadband penetration rate in the world.[1] The 74 different products manufactured by Korea are ranked top in global market share.[2] Unfortunately, despite all of these economic indicators that signal Korea's place in the world market, Korea is still relatively unknown to foreigners.

South Korea began to make a name for itself with its economic growth in the 1970-80s. It successfully hosted the Asian Games in 1986 and the Seoul Olympics in 1988. Korea then went onto co-host the World Cup with Japan in 2002 and made it to the final four against all odds. In 2010, Korea successfully hosted and presided over the G20 Summits in Seoul. The 2010 G20 Summit in Seoul was the first summits to be held outside of a G7 country. These international events, coupled with recent cultural phenonmenons such as K-pop and Korean soap operas, have all contributed increasing Korea's presence in the world today.

Now, let us talk about Korea's economic breakthrough. In 1960, Korea ranked 119th out of 120 as the poorest country in the world, but in 50 short years, Korea was able to rise to ranking 15th in GDP. Currently, South Korea is a member of OECD (Organization for Economic Co-operation and Development) and has become a sponsor to help other nations in need. For example, Korea is a global partner of the international NGO organization called Compassion, which helps impoverished children in 26 developing and underdeveloped countries around the world. The organization was founded in 1952 by an American named Everett Swanson to initially aid war orphans in Korea during the Korean War. Now, the organization helps more than a million children around the world with 11 global partners with its headquarters in Colorado Springs, Colorado.

In just 50 years, South Korea has transformed from a country in need of aid to a country that offers aid.

3 General Information about Korea

A. General Information

South Korea is located in Far East of Asia and is officially called the Republic of Korea. Its capital is Seoul and the official language is Korean.

The national flag is called *Taegeukgi*. It has a white background with a *taegeuk* in the center and four black trigrams, one in each corner. The white background of the flag represents brightness, purity, peace and loving nature of traditional Koreans. The *taegeuk* symbol in the center consists of negative (blue) and positive (red) which symbolizes the harmonious interaction of *yin* and *yang* of the universe — the idea that all things are created and developed by this harmonious interaction. Additionally, the four trigrams stand for the sky, earth, water and fire.

B. Location

The Korean Peninsula is located in the northeastern part of the Asian continent, between China and Japan. The size of the peninsula is about 220,000 square kilometers and is slightly smaller than the UK or Romania. However, Korea is divided between North and South Korea; South Korea alone spans around 100,000 square kilometers.

South Korea's population in 2010 was 48,580,293 and ranked 3rd in the world in population density.[3] It is a small country that is home to a large population. Korea's native population consists of a single ethnic group, but with a recent rise in foreign workers, the number of foreigners in the country reached 589,532 in 2010, amounting 1.2 percent of the total population.[4]

C. Capital

Seoul is the capital of South Korea. Seoul is located close to the North Korean border and is only about 25 miles from the DMZ (Demilitarized Zone). This may be nerve wrecking in the eyes of foreigners, but those living in Seoul have minimal fears. Seoul serves as the center of South Korea's politics, administration, economy, social functions, culture, and education and is home to 20.2 percent of the nation's population.[5] Although it accounts for only 0.6 percent of South Korea's land mass, Seoul generates 21 percent of the country's GDP.[6]

With headquarters of large corporation such as Samsung, LG, Hyundai, Kia, SK and Doosan, Seoul has become a major business hub as well.

D. Currency

The monetary unit of South Korea is Won. KRW is the official symbol for Korean Won in the international market. 100 won is equivalent to 5.6 British pence, 9 US cents, and .064 of a euro.

South Korea has monetary bills in 50,000 won, 10,000 won, 5,000 won and 1,000 won denominations. In addition to the most commonly used 100 won and 500 won coins, Korea has rarely used 50 won and 10 won coins.

E. Climate

Korea has four distinct seasons. Springs are warm, summers are hot and humid, falls are cool, and winters are cold. The average annual temperature is generally between 10 to 16°C and the average temperature in August, the hottest month of the year, ranges from

23 to 27°C. The coldest month is January, with temperatures from −6 to −7°C. The hottest temperatures in the summer are slightly over 30°C, and the coldest temperatures in the winter can be as low as −20°C.[7]

F. Religion

Because South Korea advocates freedom of religion, there are a variety of religions such as Buddhism, Christianity, Confucianism, Islam, and shamanism, as well as many other religions. Buddhism influences most of the people in the country because of its long history in the nation, followed by Christianity, and Confucianism. Confucianism can be considered as a way of life more than a religion and is deeply rooted in Korean manners, public sentiment, and attitudes toward life. It is also interesting that some shamanistic elements can be found in Buddhism, Christianity, and Catholicism — in an essence a mixture of pagan and modern religion can be found in Korea.

Shamanism has influenced all of South Korea's culture, religion, politics, art and custom at one time or another. Korea's shamanistic rituals give unity to Koreans' sense of ethnicity and community. Without understanding shamanism embedded in Korean culture, one cannot understand the way Koreans think. Also, shamanism was the first indigenous folk religion in Korea. It is not known when exactly shamanism was first introduced to Korea, but it is clear it is deeply rooted in Korea. The country's founding myth, the legend of *Dangun*, is based on shamanism.

The *Dangun* Myth

Dangun's father was *Hwanung*, the son of the King of Heaven. His mother was originally a bear who prayed to *Hwanung* for her to become a human. *Hwanung* told her wish would be granted if she only ate garlic and mugwort for 100 days, and this she did. After being transformed into a woman, she prayed for a son. So, *Hwanung* took her as his wife and she bore him a son, *Dangun*. *Dangun* founded the kingdom of *Gojoseon* in 2333 BC and later built the walled city of *Asadal* (near Pyongyang in North Korea).

G. Economic Situation

Since we will discuss South Korea's economy in a later chapter, we will only briefly review some general economic indicators.

In 2010, Korean GDP per capita was the world's 34th highest and when adjusted for purchasing power parity, ranked 26th amounting to $30,000. According to the International Monetary Fund's (IMF) forecast, the estimated 2010 GDP of Korea exceeded $1 trillion, ranking the nation 15th out of 184 countries for two consecutive years (2009-2011). The 2010 GDP per capita was at $20,591. This ranks Korea as 34th in the world for 2010 and puts the GDP per capita at $20,000 for the first time in three years. GDP per capita was $21,653 in 2007.

Korean trade dependence has remained in the 50-60 percentiles since 2000, but has sharply increased with recent financial crisis. Korea's trade dependence marked 62.4 percent in 2000, 57.8 percent in 2001, 54.6 percent in 2002, 57.9 percent in 2003, 66.2 percent in 2004, 64.6 percent in 2005, and 69.4 percent in 2007. However, in 2008, there was a 30 percent increase, reaching to an average of 90 percent. Since then, Korea's trade dependence has continued to remain high at 82.4 percent in 2009, and 85 percent in 2010. This can be interpreted as a sign of Korean economy's vulnerability to external shocks.[8]

In 2010, 16.2 percent of South Korea's population was 0-14 years old, 72.4 percent was 15-64 years old, and 11.4 percent was over 64. It is projected that the percentage of the population over 64 will increase from 11.0 percent to 38.2 percent by 2050, and those over 80 years of age will increase from 2.0 percent (this is less than the 4.3 percent average for developed countries) to 14.5 percent in 2050 (higher than developed country average of 9.5 percent).[9]

By 2000, Korea had already become an "aging society." Moreover, the aging of the population is expected to progress faster than that of most countries and is projected to constitute 14.3 percent of the population by 2018.

Now, let us consider the productive population. According to OECD statistics, the productive population of Korea is 73.1 percent of the entire population, the highest percentage among 34 OECD countries. South Korea is the only OECD country where the productive proportion of the population exceeds 70 percent. However, although this ratio is projected to rise to 73.4 percent in 2015, it is expected to fall below 70 percent by 2024 to an estimated 69.2 percent. The main reasons for South Korea's rapid productive population decline in comparison to other countries are most likely due to low birth rates and an increasingly aging population.

5
History of Korea

1 The Settlement of Koreans

It is estimated that Koreans settled on the Korean Peninsula at least 30,000 years ago. These early settlers were nomads who migrated from the northwest. They were similar to the Mongols of Central Asia in particular and shared similar faith, shamanism. Many theories claim that Koreans are a mixture of a Northern and Southeastern Asian race. However, Koreans consider themselves as a single race.[10]

2 Beginnings of the Country

The Bronze Age in Korea is known to have started around 2000 BC and the Iron Age that followed started around the year 300 BC. Korea first took the form of a country in 2333 BC and went by the name of *Gojoseon*. In 37 BC, *Goguryeo* succeeded *Gojoseon* and this is the name from which the current name "Korea" was derived.

3 Three Kingdoms Period

Baekje (18 BC to AD 660) and *Silla* (57 BC to AD 935) kingdoms were established around the same time as *Goguryeo*. These three kingdom's borders intersected not far from modern-day Seoul. *Goguryeo*'s territory covered what is now Manchuria. It was a formidable country that threatened China. These three kingdoms each traded with China and learned China's advanced science, religion, social institutions, and culture. *Baekje* went on to relay such knowledge to Japan. The terrain of the peninsula that was divided into three kingdoms still remains the cause of regionalism in Korea today.

During this period, *Silla*'s Buddhist artwork flourished and was used in many of its buildings and artifacts that still remain today. The *Seokgul* Grotto and the *Bulguk* Temple represent the peak of *Silla*'s Buddhist architecture and other ornate artifacts such as crowns, bracelets and rings boast artful craftsmanship.

4 Unification of the Three Kingdoms

In 668 AD, *Silla* combined forces with China's *Tang* Dynasty to destroy *Baekje* and *Goguryeo* and unify the peninsula. However, because *Silla* was assisted by the *Tang* Dynasty, *Silla* had to forfeit most of *Goguryeo*'s former territory to *Tang* in exchange.

Around this time in 698 AD, a former *Goguryeo* general established the *Balhae* kingdom in the hopes of resurrecting *Goguryeo*, but the country did not last and was soon destroyed. Even today, it is unclear how the destruction of *Balhae* came about, but a volcanic eruption of Mt. *Baekdu* is assumed to be the cause.

5 The *Goryeo* Dynasty

The *Goryeo* Dynasty was established after the collapse of the *Silla* Dynasty.

Buddhism, reached its peak during the *Goryeo* Dynasty. The Tripitaka Koreana, a national treasure today, was created at this time.

The *Goryeo* Dynasty was plagued by serious conflict between the King and its military officials. Towards the end of the *Goryeo* Dynasty, the weakness of the king allowed military officials to gain more power and General Lee Seong-gye eventually overthrew the dynasty.

Great advancements in science were made in the *Goryeo* Dynasty: the world's first book was printed in 1377 by using metal movable type called the *Jikji*, years before Gutenberg invented the movable metal type in 1450. Also, the world famous ceramics known as *Goryeo* Celadon were invented during this time and are still considered a world cultural heritage.

The Tripitaka Koreana (*Palman Daejanggyeong*)

The Tripitaka Koreana (*Palman Daejanggyeong*), meaning the "Eighty-Thousand Tripitaka," is the world's oldest and most complete collection of Buddhist Scriptures. This collection of Buddhist scriptures, called Tripitaka, was created in the 13th century and is carved onto 81,258 wooden printing blocks, giving its name the "Eighty-Thousand Tripitaka." It is designated as a UNESCO World Heritage today.

6 The *Joseon* Dynasty

As mentioned, General Lee Seong-gye destroyed *Goryeo* and established the *Joseon* Dynasty. This is when the capital was moved to what is now Seoul. During the *Joseon* Dynasty, the corrupted ideology of Buddhism was rejected, and in an attempt to justify his rise to power, Lee Seong-gye forced Confucianism to the country. It served as the national ideology until the *Joseon* Dynasty met its end.

The most well-known *Joseon* kings is King Sejong who is one of the most revered figures amongst Koreans. Not only was King Sejong a venerable ruler, he was also one of Korea's best scientists as well. He invented *Hangul*, the Korean writing system, and numerous scientific instruments such as the sundial, the water clock, and rain gauge. His statue stands proudly in front of *Gwanghwamun*, the main gate of the *Gyeongbok* Palace in Seoul.

Japan invaded Korea for the first time during *Joseon* Dynasty. Previously, Japanese pirates stole goods from Koreans in the coastal areas, but this was the first time that Koreans experienced a national threat from the Japanese. In 1592, more than 150,000 Japanese troops arrived in the southern coastal city of Busan, which ignited a war with Japan that lasted seven years.

During this war, *Joseon*'s naval commander Admiral Yi Sun-sin used his turtle-shaped ship along with masterful strategies to defeat the Japanese navy. Even to this day, Admiral Yi is one of the most respected figures in Korean history and a statue in his honor stands in the heart of downtown Seoul. Next to him is a statue of one of the "turtle ships" that he used in battle. There is a view this turtle ship was the world's first iron-armoured warship and is in the shape of a primitive submarine.

During the late *Joseon* Dynasty, the kingship began to weaken rapidly. In an attempt to regain power, the king and his officials adopted an isolationist policy, which only further weakened their power. They refused to accept the advanced science and social institutions of other countries and reverted to the past which only made *Joseon* an attractive target to the rising world powers with ambitions for expansion.

7 The Japanese Colonial Period

In the late 19th century, the Japanese sought to gain a foothold in China along with European nations. Consequently, Japan put great pressure on Korea as the starting point of its advance into China.

In 1905, the Korea-Japan Protectorate Treaty was signed and the *Joseon*'s sovereignty was taken by the Japanese. In 1910, Korea became a colony of Japan. The 20th century opened with Japanese occupation of Korea; despite tremendous efforts by the Koreans to regain national independence, Korea remained Japan's colony.

8 Republic of Korea

Korea gained its independence after Japan was defeated in World War II. However Korea became a divided nation after a political strife; the South allied with the United States and the North allied with the Soviet Union. South Korea's national independence took place in 1945 at the end of World War II but true independence was only established at the end of 1948, when US troops withdrew and a democratic government was elected by South Korea.

In 1950, with the help of the Soviet Union and China, North Korea invaded South Korea resulting in Korean War for three years. The war was fought with the help of the United Nations and a truce was signed in 1953. To this day, South Korea and North Korea remain the sole divided country in the world where the possibility of war still lingers. South Korea was devastated by the war, which caused widespread destruction of its production facilities and infrastructure. This led to South Korea's demise as one of the world's poorest countries in 1953.

Today, the economic strength of South Korea is 19 times that of North Korea[11] and with North Korea unable to feed its citizens without South Korea's help, the chances of another civil war is slim to none. Nevertheless, North Korea continues to provoke South Korea in various ways, such as firing a South Korean patrol ship in South Korean waters in 2010. These incidents are viewed by many as North Korea's desperate attempt to threaten South Korea for more aid and gain leverage in international negotiations, rather than to actually start a war.

6

Korea's Economy

1 Korea's Economic Position

The Korean economy proves that it is possible for an impoverished country to prosper into a developed country. The country faced many disadvantages including a lack of natural resources, limited land from geographical division, and a dense, small population not large enough to sustain economies of scale. It may have seemed impossible for Korea to rise to world's 15th largest economy, given these circumstances. However, Korea has made the impossible, possible. It was not too long ago when the country was struggling to battle starvation and people were eating tree roots to merely survive, but the Republic of Korea has risen as world's number one in Internet penetration and as prominent producer of mobile phones, semiconductors, and ships; Korea became an undisputed leader in some of the world's leading industries.

We will now describe Korea's economic history chronologically to see how far it has come since its liberation from Japan in 1945.

2 1945-1961: the Change from a Dependent Economy to an Independent Economy

The most important event that occurred between 1945 and 1961 is the division of the country. Korea's liberation from Japan in the August of 1945 helped change its economy from a once dependent economy to an independent one. However, the civil division left the South with agricultural land and the North with industrial resources. South Korea was left with 70 percent of the nation's agricultural capacity and North Korea approximately 30 percent, while South Korea had 30 percent of the nation's industrial facilities and North Korea 70 percent.[12] Ultimately, South Korea was left as an underdeveloped, agricultural nation.

During this time, foreign aid, especially from the US, sustained the Koreans and helped the South Korea's industrial production activities. South Korea's economic development during 1945 to 1948 started with the US military aid to South Korea after World War II. Foreign aid continued until the early 1960 for nearly fifteen years, leaving South Korea largely dependent. In a survey conducted by UN, of 120 countries in the world, Bangladesh was ranked as the poorest, while South Korea came in as the second poorest nation in the world.

3 1962-1981: Overcoming Hunger and Developing into a Prosperous Country

From 1962 to 1981, the average annual economic growth rate exploded to 8.29 percent and per capita GNP (Gross National Product) growth to 5.715 percent.[13] This greatly exceeded the world average at the time. During this period of rapid growth, 1980 was the only year that Korea had negative growth rate. Korea maintained positive growth during 1974 and 1975 while the rest of the world suffered recession from the oil shock of 1973. From 1962 to 1981,

Korea's economy was characterized by consistent high growth rate.

The economic boom of this time was spearheaded by Park Chung-hee, who seized political power in a 1961 coup d'état and laid out a strict economic development strategy.

The economic expansion was accompanied by a transformation of the industrial structure. In the 1970s, the Korean government fostered the chemical industries. From 1962 to 1981, a multi-phase economic development plan was carried out. Under this plan, development increased in the secondary and tertiary industries and light and heavy chemical industries increased in the industrial sector. At this time, government support of small and medium-sized businesses decreased while large conglomerates emerged.

In the 1960s and 1970s, the Korean labor force played a critical role in economic growth. South Korea reached a population of approximately 29 million in 1965, which increased to 38 million in 1980. During that time the economically active population had increased faster than the total population. In 1965, the economically active population was nearly 8.9 million, and by 1980, it had increased to about 14.4 million.[14] Such rapid increase of economically active population was primarily due to the changes in the population structure.

The change of population structure produced an increase in the working population in proportion to the total population, as well as the growth in the female labor force. The proportion of women in the labor force increased from 36.5 percent in 1965 to 41.6 percent in 1980 and has become an increasingly important factor in the Korean economy. By now women in the labor force have risen to 57.1 percent.[15]

Some Koreans went abroad and started sending foreign currency back to Korea, which helped the Korean government in securing funding for economic development.

In the 1960s, many twentysomething Koreans left for Germany to become miners and nurses. This emigration to Germany was Korea's first major emigration period in Korean history. The wages of the Korean miners and nurses in West Germany provided Korea with 150 million marks (about 30 million dollars), used to pay for industrial development imports.[16] From the time the first Korean nurse set foot in Germany in 1966 until 1977, a total of 10,226 nurses went to work in Germany.[17] Also, since the first 123 Korean miners arrived in Germany in 1963 to 1978, about 7,900 miners went to Germany. When 500 miners were to be sent in 1963, nearly 46,000 Koreans volunteered, raising the acceptance rate to 1:92. We can only imagine how hard it was to get by in Korea for so many citizens to apply for immigration to Germany. The money that these workers sent back to Korea was estimated to be around 50 million dollars and made up 2 percent of Korea's GNP at the time.

Also, the Arab oil producers who became rich during the oil crisis in the 1970s, started major constructions and civil engineering projects that were carried out by Korean companies. Korean construction companies were favored because they were cheap labor, had good workmanship, and completed projects within a short period of time. This is referred to as the construction boom of the Middle East. During this time, South Korea was able to gain large amounts of foreign exchange that served as an indispensable asset in promoting economic development. From the Sahara Desert to Antarctica, Koreans did not hesitate to work in harsh environments to help achieve the South Korea of today.

Sending troops to the war in Vietnam also played a crucial role in Korea's economic growth. Korea deployed troops to Vietnam from 1964 to 1973. At the time, Korea's economy was considered so underdeveloped and impoverished that they could not even fathom overseas expansion of their corporations. However, Korea was able to earn approximately 1 billion dollars by deploying troops to Vietnam, thereby gaining valuable foreign exchange for economic development.

During this period, a social reform movement called the *Saemaul* (meaning new village in Korean) Movement took place. The movement became the engine of modernization and the fundamental basis of the economic boom. The *Saemaul* Movement was intended "for a good life" and was advocated by President Park Chung-hee in 1970. He proposed that farmers, organizations and community leaders cooperate in self-help efforts to boost productivity. He organized the movement around a voluntary, cooperative body. This campaign started in 1971 and became nationwide by 1973.

The *Saemaul* Movement quickly improved agricultural competitiveness through the voluntary participation, building a sense of community, and confidence. This movement was the driving force of modernization in Korean society, both in homes and workplace.

Current UN Secretary-General Ban Ki-moon recommended the UN to learn more about the *Saemaul* Movement for the impoverished African nations. The UN showed such a keen interest in this movement that they selected it for the UN in Africa to eliminate poverty. The *Saemaul* Movement has now been adopted by 74 countries and other developing countries continue to show interests in applying it.

From 1960s to 1980s, the size of the educated workforce increased with people's keen desire for education. In addition, there was an increase in investment, which played a key role in economic growth and as well as a rapid increase in domestic savings.

4 1982-1987: South Korea's Economy Seeks Help

Although Korea saw great economic growth with a 10 percent annual growth rate during the 1960s and 1970s, it faced economic troubles in the 1980s due to political and social strife.[18] Military coups and ensuing dictatorships, followed by protests for democracy threatened the country's newly found stability, but national and corporate efforts eventually helped Korea regain its stability.

During the 1960s and 1970s, agriculture and fishing industries waned while the manufacturing and service industries flourished. This tendency continued into 1980s. As the economy grew, industries based on manual labor were passed onto Southeast Asian countries and China, and were replaced by industries requiring more skilled labor.

5 1988-1997: Economic Development, an Overheated Economy, and the IMF Bailout

Economic growth slowed in the late 1980s and Korea had a large trade deficit in 1990 and 1991. This was largely due to an increase in domestic demand while the competitiveness of Korea's export market declined.

International economic conditions deteriorated as well, threatening Korea's continued economic development. Furthermore, international oil prices rose sharply due to the instability in the Middle East in the 1990s.

Since the early 1980s, Korea moved toward a more liberal economic policy along with a more democratic government. Just after the government declared democracy in 1987, the working class rose up against their condition, skyrocketing the cost of labor. This further exacerbated the declining national competitive edge.

In the 1990s, the poorly managed country's foreign exchange reserves, excessive short-term borrowings, and the failure of the exchange rate management policy resulted in a foreign exchange crisis. This ultimately led to the IMF bailout in December of 1997.

IMF Bailout and Recovery

The International Monetary Fund (IMF) was established for the purpose of stabilizing world trade. On November 21, 1997, when Korea could not meet its foreign debt obligations, it accepted the stringent, economic reforms imposed by the IMF as the conditions for bailout to prevent national bankruptcy. On August 23, 2001, Korea fully reimbursed the IMF for the bailout and was thereby able to publicly terminate the IMF-imposed reforms.

6 1998-Present: Overcoming IMF and Change

The depreciation of the won led to a severe crash in the stock and real estate markets. In January of 1997, 1 US dollar was equivalent to 840 won, but by December 26, 1998, 1 US dollar reached

1860 won. As of June 1998, the stock market index dropped to 277 from 800. The IMF bailout was a serious threat to Korea that caused changes in both administration and existing social norms.

Moreover, the IMF bailout brought about a series of liquidations of conglomerates that were no longer competitive. In June of 1998, 55 companies announced liquidation and in 1999, Daewoo Group went bankrupt despite massive government support. Large-scale mergers and acquisitions ensued for banks and many corporations were sold to foreign companies at bargain prices.

Analysts have stated that Korea's IMF crisis was largely due to companies that monopolized the market. Since then, the Fair Trade Commission and the Financial Supervisory Commission were formed to address this problem. Development policy reforms were also emphasized.

The Gold Gathering Movement and the IMF

During this period the entire nation worked together to gather and donate gold to the government, which were then used to pay back Korea's foreign debt. This movement promoted unity among Koreans during a time of hardship and received national attention. At the time of IMF bailout, the foreign debt of the Republic of Korea reached about 30.4 billion US dollars. A total of about 3.5 million people nationwide participated in this movement and contributed around 227 tons of gold to repay this debt.

On August 23, 2001, Korea fully reimbursed the IMF for the bailout. The debt of 19.5 billion US dollars was paid off three years sooner than planned. Economic indicators also showed significant improvement and foreign exchange reserves ranked number five in the world by 2010. These results definitely distinguish South Korea from other Asian countries' experiences with IMF bailouts.

The IMF provided a means for South Korea to improve its economic condition and South Korea was able to capitalize on the crisis as an opportunity to rise again. Nevertheless, the economy has been in recession since the end of 2000 and the restructuring of corporations and financial markets is still on-going.

In 2007, the US subprime mortgage crisis started a series of recessions around the world and the US has been experiencing one of the longest recessions since the Great Depression. Countries like Korea that had invested in the US financial market since the 1970s, incurred heavy losses. Although Korea was able to secure the value of the won through a cross-certification policy in foreign exchange value and the stability in the foreign exchange market had been restored, it still experienced an economic downturn until 2010 as the unemployment rate rose and the domestic market slowed down.

Korea's economic growth in 2011 was not as strong as 2010. Economic growth was expected to be 3.7 percent lower than in 2010 due to the decrease in worldwide, overall economic growth. In addition to the global economic slowdown, there was a decline in export growth, real estate, and construction industries. Since 2010, the production of semiconductors and the growth of the automotive industry have slowed while future market conditions remain uncertain. However, Korea is still on the forefront of semiconductor production, shipbuilding, high-tech industries, steel and automobile industry, as well as other sectors.

7

Characteristics of Koreans

Now, let us consider some Korean cultural characteristics, the foundation for Koreans' behavior. The following are some typical Korean characteristics.

1 The Pursuit of Tradition (Purity)

Koreans place emphasis on tradition and purity. By tradition, we mean something that has not been changed or mixed with other elements; in other words, the purity has not been affected. The importance of tradition stems from the rejection of any element that has been tainted. Because of their fondness for maintaining tradition, change is not perceived positively and diversity is rarely pursued in Korea.

In Korean corporations, relocating, mergering, or restructuring departments may have unseen resistance and side effects. This phenomenon may exist in any country, but it is often far more severe in Korea than in other countries. There is a strong tendency for Korean workers to settle down in a company they have worked at for a long time. So when circumstances call for a change, they first reject it from fear and insecurity. For example, a newly structured organization with new staff would cause anxiety to many Koreans. When such anxieties grow, it disrupts corporate unity, causes inefficiencies and produces detachment from the company.

Therefore, when circumstances lead to a change, it is important to announce it beforehand and explain the necessity for the change. It is also important to train the employees for the new tasks while promoting a spirit of challenge and inspiring creativity. Unfortunately, Korea's labor unions are often very radical and are known to display socialist tendencies, making it difficult to gain their consent for change.

2 Equality and Hierarchy

"All men are equal."

For Westerners, the concept of equality does not mean equal distribution, but means equal opportunities. However, for Koreans, equality refers to equal results. This kind of reasoning may seem irrational and confusing to foreigners. For example, it might seem irrational for two workers who produce different results to receive the same incentives.

Koreans judge equality based on what can be seen by others. Therefore, the desire to be as good as someone else, or to be better than others, is very strong. The positive aspect of this is that it promotes motivation. The lower class is motivated to move up in social class by pursuing higher education because education is the foundation for upward mobility. "Those with higher education are smarter" is a common, longstanding notion in Korea. Therefore, equality came to be defined as "doing as well as others." This served as a key contributing factor in Korea's rapid economic development.

Ironically, Koreans seek equality, yet are fixated on hierarchy. Koreans tend to feel comfortable when a hierarchy is formed within their group. In Korea, hierarchy is distinct even among families and there are many titles that clearly demonstrate this hierarchy. The lowest person in a hierarchy must refer to those in the higher ranks by title and never by name, regardless of age. If the person does not use these titles then he or she is considered to be uneducated and rude. In Korea, it is still important between parent and child, old and young, senior and junior, and teacher and student to maintain hierarchy in their relationships. These hierarchies heavily influence social interactions in classrooms, meetings or conferences.

It may be baffling to Westerners but in the past Korean hierarchy determined who walks in the left and right sides of the road. Until the end of the 19th century, noblemen travelled on the right side of the road while the peasants and animals walked on the left side of the road. Those that did not comply suffered grave consequences. This practice still lingers in Korean culture and it is viewed as rude to offer or accept a drink with the left or "inferior" hand. Even in such trivial matters, Koreans place importance on tradition and hierarchy.

3 Nepotism

We will take a look at nepotism, greatly valued by Koreans. As mentioned, Koreans try to establish common ground when first meeting someone. This is the same when conducting business. When meeting someone for the first time in a business setting, Koreans do not immediately talk about business but rather try to establish common ground from which business can be discussed. Questions regarding hometowns, current place of residence, prior visits to Korea and hobbies are asked in attempts to establish a common ground.

So, how do Koreans categorize other people? The types of relationships that Koreans consider to be most important are kinship, school, and hometown. These three categories are very influential in Korea. Of these, the most important of all relationships to Koreans is kin.

In Korea, genealogy is very important. Each Korean household has a family tree, or *jokbo*. The *jokbo* is like a history book that indicates kinship in a household based on surname. In other words, *jokbo* is a book that has details of each family's ancestors recorded. In the past, it was said that the first thing to grab when your house was on fire was the *jokbo*, for it was considered a family treasure.

Kinship between two people is recognized only if they share the origin, not just the surname. For example, there are Kims of many different origins, such as the Gimhae Kim line and the Gwangsan Kim line. Because the two different Kim lineages have different bloodlines, not all Kims are considered kin. In Korea, sharing the same surname and origin as someone else will begin a relationship on a great footing, even if you do not know the other person well.

In modern Korean society, being alumni from certain universities often entitles one to a certain social class. Graduating from an elite university guarantees a life in the middle class or above. In addition, connections made at these universities can be influential in work life. Recently, however, organizations do not look favorably on boasting about educational ties. This is because such ties often have adverse effects on promoting diversity and transparency within an organization. Nevertheless, the Korean society still operates on the basis of relationships established at universities, despite being relatively toned down in recent years.

Korea is a fairly small country, yet hometown is a very salient notion for its people. Historically, it dates back to the period of the Three Kingdoms, *Goguryeo*, *Baekje* and *Silla* (37 BC to AD 935) when the Korean Peninsula was divided into three kingdoms.

When people meet for the first time and realize that they are from the same hometown, they instantly feel closer and may even converse in their local dialect. These types of regional relationships have long affected Korean politics. Regional boundaries form the basis for political parties and government administrations rise based on regional support. Corporations are no exception and had a tendency to hire employees from the executives' hometowns. Fortunately, such hiring practices have greatly declined due to promotion of equality in hiring.

4 Sense of Urgency.

The ancestors of Koreans were nomads who later settled into farming. Koreans have retained the nomadic tendency of being fast paced ("*bbali bbali*"), resourceful, and hot-temper. Koreans typically has fiery tempers and often do not think things through carefully or rationally. Because of this, Koreans are often considered to have a similar disposition to Italians or the Irish. When describing Koreans, foreigners often use the phrase, "*bbali bbali* (hurry-hurry)." This is a testament to the foreigners' perception that Koreans are quite hurried.

This sense of urgency supposedly led to the rapid Korean advancement into digitalization. Koreans initially had many complaints about Internet speed (or lack of it), to which the carriers had to quickly respond. Currently, Korean Internet connections rank as the world's fastest and most stable. Fashion-conscious Koreans strive to obtain new digital devices that are at the cutting-edge in communication networks. Laptops, smart phones and high-tech digital devices that provide convenience and speed seem to cater to the ancient nomadic taste for convenience and speed.

5 Cohesion

There is a Korean ad with the expression, "Nothing is impossible in Korea!" In fact, many use this expression in real life. Unfortunately, such attitude can lead to negative effects, such as pestering one's employees relentlessly until desired results are met. On the other hand, this attitude can be seen as tenacity to overcome a challenge rather than deeming something impossible.

This Korean energy to unite and work together cohesively to achieve goals is unique in comparison to many developed nations that favor individualism. This cohesiveness shines in times of crisis. When invaded by enemies, Korea has always resisted and fought till the end. When Japan colonized Korea in the 20th century, Koreans continued to resist and fought against the Japanese through various underground independence movements.

Let us consider another example that illustrates the cohesion of Koreans. In 2002, Korea cohosted the World Cup with Japan. Korea advanced to the final 8, then the final 4, with increasing foreign media's attention. But what received most attention were the cheering Korean citizens also known as the Red Devils. The entire nation cheered on their team dressed in red, showing a united front to the entire world.

Family-oriented Koreans rise as one cohesive group to help organizations or the country. During the country's financial crisis (IMF crisis) in 1998, everyone in Korea gathered gold to repay the bailout money and free the country from the restrictive IMF policies. Similarly, when a company undergoes financial difficulties, employees will often return salaries and try to revive the company. In such instances, Koreans equate their state with their own family and in the face of a common goal, and the effect of cohesion can be quite intimidating. Therefore, leaders, who can leverage this trait, both in state and in organizations, will be successful in Korea.

6 "*Jung*"

We will now consider a term special to Koreans, "*Jung*." Koreans are people with a lot of "*Jung*." "*Jung*" refers to the warm affection felt between people. It is the combination of the English words, love, friendship, warm feeling, favor, affection, trust, and commitment.

"*Jung*" does not form instantaneously, but slowly, over a long period of time as people get together regularly and become closer through conversations. It is not a feeling of like or dislike toward the other person, but is created through repeated contact and a continued relationship.

"*Jung*" can be considered a mental bond, as by an unseen force. "*Jung*" can be formed in any relationships; between couples, during parenthood, with friends, neighbors, colleagues, the elderly and the young, teachers and students. Usually, when a person is said to have a lot of "*Jung*," it means they have warm and kind character. "*Jung*" is a warm feeling and does not carry the intensity of love. However, just because "*Jung*" is expressed more subtly, it is not a lesser feeling than love. It may not be as explosive as passionate love, but "*Jung*" has a strong sense of longing for others and relationships. If love is a dynamic concept, "*Jung*" is static.

After the devastating earthquake in Japan in 2011, Koreans sent volunteers as well as donations for relief supplies. Even though anti-Japanese sentiments widely prevail in Korea today, its "*Jung*" for its neighboring country allowed Korea to overlook such feelings and aid Japan. Giving up seats to the elderly or to pregnant women in subways and enthusiastically helping friends in need are some behaviors underlined by "*Jung*."

7 "*Han*"

"*Han*" is a concept that is quite difficult to explain to foreigners. "*Han*" refers to an emotion that is a combination of anger, sorrow, regret, and self-pity that arises when something you so desperately wanted to achieve could not be accomplished. "*Han*" does not form suddenly but by harboring such emotions in one's heart for a long time.

Under the Confucian values, men, women and different social class had to strictly abide by distinct social roles. This prevented many from achieving their own personal goals such as not being able to get a higher education because of low social status, not being able to call your father "father" because of having a low-class mother, or not being able to love freely due to class restrictions.

Such examples of "*Han*" can still be found. Let us consider an example of a famous singer in Korea. The singer was raised in a very poor family. His mother eventually died of an illness after living a hard life, although she could have been cured had they had the money. After the singer's mother died, he built up "*Han*" within and worked hard to become a famous singer in Korea and in the US. He still feels "*Han*" about the fact that his mother had to die the way she did, but no matter how successful he is now, he cannot do anything for her because she is gone. However, that same "*Han*" is probably the motivating factor that makes him work harder.

Koreans have not just harbored "*Han*" in their heart but transformed it into various forms of art such as poetry, literature, painting and music. The most famous of such works bearing "*Han*" is the classic Korean song, 'Arirang.' The song 'Arirang' laments the departure of a loved one. It sings that, as you watch your love leave, you hope that your love will injure his/her foot not after 3 miles. The song captures the anguish of a person not being able to hold onto a loved one. By expressing "*Han*" as art, "*Han*" is no longer a negative feeling, but it is now a part of the Korean culture.

8 Saving Face

There isn't anyone without pride, but Koreans consider saving face and pride to be exceptionally important. Saving face is an Asian concept of self-esteem. Pride is often a question of self-perception and how valuable one considers oneself. But saving face, on the contrary, is about how others may perceive you, which can be called self-conscious pride.

There are a few Korean adages that highlight the psychology of saving face. One adage says, "Drink cold water and pick your teeth." This is about using a toothpick after drinking water to pretend that you've had a satisfying meal in front of others — therefore saving one's face about their impending poverty. The noblemen of ancient times were especially accustomed to saving face.

Here is another adage: "No matter how cold, one will not get warm in another's fire." This adage illustrates that a proud nobleman will never get warm by sneaking to another's fire, even though it may be more beneficial for the nobleman to forego saving face and seek warmth.

Some Koreans buy expensive cars, wedding gifts, or entertain guests at expensive restaurants all in the name of "saving face." This attitude may stem from the past when Korea had a class-oriented authoritarian society. Saving face allows a person to communicate and interact with others according to their status. Saving face ultimately determined the type of basic etiquette that people used in olden times. Today, rather than saving face, being practical is becoming more common, particularly to the younger generation. However, because saving face has long been established as part of Korean culture, the notion remains, though it has modernized in recent times.

Summary of Chapter 1

1. Globalizing and Globalization

- In a globalized world, working together with other nationals or ethnic groups is very common. Globalization is accelerating and in order to have a successful global business we need to have a better understanding of cultural differences.
- Effective communication is critical in overcoming cultural differences for multinational companies.

2. Management and Communication

- Management unites people with different skills and knowledge toward a common goal by combining various functions like marketing, finance, production, sales, and R&D. In this process, the role of management is to enhance the benefits and compensate for the shortcomings of the workers.
- Communication is typically defined as the social process of an individual, group, or organization exchanging or sharing messages and information. Effective communication is critical for multinational companies.
- It is important that people of different cultures and languages strive to communicate accurately and in a timely manner while adapting quickly to changing circumstances and moving towards a common goal.

3. First Meeting with Koreans

- When Koreans meet someone for the first time, they are most interested in the other person's age, position/title, and where they are from.
- When speaking about themselves, Koreans have a tendency to define themselves as part of a group.
- When meeting a foreigner, Koreans are very curious of the other person's ethnicity and nationality. Koreans often want to stereotype foreigners. They also want to connect with the foreigner by finding a common ground.

4. General Information about Korea

- The Korean Peninsula is located in the northeastern part of the Asian continent, between China and Japan. Korea's capital is Seoul and Korean is the official language.
- The GDP of Korea exceeded $1 trillion and ranked 15th globally in 2010. The GDP per capita was ranked 34th in the world at $20,591 in 2010.

5. History of Korea

- Korea first established itself as a nation in 2333 BC and went by the name of *Gojoseon*. It boasts a history of over 5,000 years.
- In 1950, North Korea invaded South Korea with the help of the Soviet Union and China, resulting in the Korean War that lasted three years. The war was fought with the help of the UN and a truce was signed in 1953. From this war, South Korea and North Korea remain the only divided country in the world today.

6. Korea's Economy

- In 1960, Korea was ranked as the second poorest country in the world.
- By implementing Economic Development Plan in 1962, Koreans created something from nothing. The country's many disadvantages included lack of natural resources, limited land, overpopulation, and geographical division, with little advantages to list. It may even seem impossible to have risen as the world's 15th largest economy, given these circumstances. However, Korea has made the impossible possible — Koreans refer this event as the "Miracle of *Han* River."

7. Characteristics of Koreans

- We've learned some Korean characteristics that are the foundations of Koreans' behaviors: the Pursuit of Tradition (Purity), Equality and Hierarchy, Nepotism, Sense of Urgency, Cohesion, "*Jung*," "*Han*," Saving Face.
- It is helpful to understand these traits in order to understand Koreans and Korean organizations in business settings.

Chapter 02

Asia and the West

1 Differences between Asian and Western Ways of Thinking

2 Comparing South Korea, China, and Japan

The world is full of diverse cultures, each of which shape how people think and behave. Especially, the difference between Asian and Western cultures is greater than you can imagine for each has originated from different ancient civilizations.

Geographically, Korea is located in Far East Asia. Hence, it is important that we understand the differences between Asians and Westerners. Also, to better understand Koreans, it is important to learn about Korea's neighbors, China and Japan.

In Chapter 2, we offer detailed explanations on the different viewpoints of Asians and Westerners and explore the sources of these differences. Lastly, we will compare the differences between the cultures of Korea, China and Japan.

1

Differences between Asian and Western Ways of Thinking

Observe the target object and the flowers in group A and B.[1] Do you think the single target flower best fits into group A or B? Why?

There is no correct answer to the question. However, when asked to many Asians and Westerners, they showed marked differences in grouping the target flower.

This is an experiment from an article titled, "Cultural preferences for formal versus intuitive reasoning," published in the academic journal *Cognitive Science*.[2] Most Asians thought that the

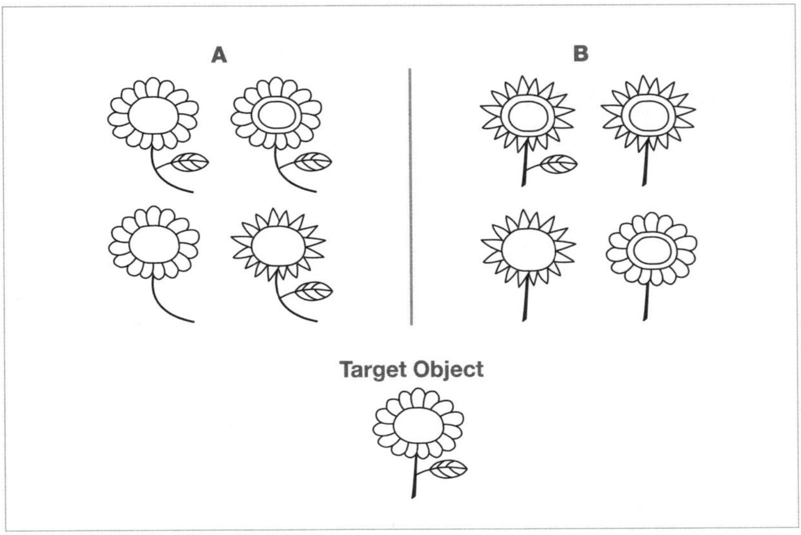

small flower belongs to group A while most Westerners thought that it belongs to group B. Even with such trivial matter, we can see that there are differences between the ways Asians and Westerners think. What is the underlying cause of such result?

In this exercise, Asians thought the target flower belongs to group A, whereas Westerners thought that it belongs to group B. Asians chose group A based on an overall similarity in appearance and Westerners chose group B because the flowers all shared straight stems.

Most of the flowers in group A have round petals, whereas most of the flowers in group B have pointy petals. Westerners focused on the shape of the stem, and categorized the target flower as group B. In other words, Asians categorized the flower based on an overall appearance while Westerners categorized it based on each variable's characteristic. This exercise also serves as evidence that Asians and Westerners categorize objects differently.

1 Differences between Asian and Western Cultures and Their Roots

As mentioned in Chapter 1, understanding the differences between Asians and Westerners have grown in its importance as globalization continues for both nations and corporations.

Failing to understand these differences can lead to serious conflict between nations or within an organization. The best way to mitigate these differences would be to first begin by respecting the different ways of thinking and behaviors. To facilitate such mutual respect, understanding the reason behind these ways of thinking is necessary.

Now, why do Asians and Westerners think and act differently? It is largely due to their uniquely different cultures. Culture is the human intellect, belief and action, collectively. Therefore, it is most appropriate to begin our understanding of the cultural differences between the East and the West by first understanding the concept of culture. Understanding the unique characteristics of a given culture can only provide superficial understanding. To gain deeper understanding of the different cultures, it is necessary to examine their similarities and differences in multiple dimensions. Moreover, it is also imperative to examine various factors that constitute the culture. This chapter is designed to examine the various characteristics of the Asian and Western cultures and learn about their differences.

First, let us take a look at the origins of these cultures. Today, approximately 1 billion people inherited intellectual heritage from Ancient Greece and 2 billion from Ancient China. The former are said to be influenced by the Western civilization and the latter by the Asian civilization.

Generally, Western culture is built on two main pillars: one pillar is Judaism and Christianity, and the other pillar is Greco-Roman tradition. On the other hand, Asian culture is supported by Taoism and Confucianism. Both cultures were formed several centuries before A.D.

While Western culture originated from Greece and continued to expand seaside through the Mediterranean, Asian culture originated from China and continued its growth continentally within East Asia. Until the two cultures met along the Pacific Ocean in the 19th century, the two cultures were virtually segregated from each other.

Western culture searched for answers to the most fundamental question of human existence and the relationship between man and nature. The answer emphasized on the concept of "separation." Greek and Roman traditions, a pillar in the Western culture, also exhibit the concept of separation. Philosophies of Socrates, Plato and Aristotle are all built on the assumption of separation of mind from body, or separation of man from nature. The conception of separation continued throughout Renaissance Europe to Descartes, the father of modern philosophy who famously proclaimed, "I think, therefore I am." Such statement illustrates the importance of mind over body. Kant's "pure reason" and Hegel's "absolute idealism" also speak to the tradition of separation of mind from body and the importance of mind in Western philosophy.

In Asia, the relationship between man and nature was conceptualized by *Tao* (way), relationships between men by benevolence, relationship between mind and body by *Liki* (理氣) philosophy. The fundamental thought underlying these relationships is harmony. The *Tao* of Asia serves a similar role to the Gods of the West in that there is a relationship between man and nature. However, the difference between the two is that *Tao* harmonizes man with nature and God separates man from nature. Harmony, an omnipresent concept of Asian culture, is best explained by *Yin-Yang* philosophy. *Yin-Yang* philosophy explains the relationship between two contrasting factors such as, light and dark, male and female, sun and moon, summer and winter, active and passive, as complementarity while Western culture characterize these with separation and conflict.

The differences between East and West date back 2500 years to ancient Greece and China. These two cradles of modern civilization differed greatly in their perspective on man and social structures, as well as philosophy and civilization.

2 Differences between Asian and Western Ways of Thinking

A. A Part of a Family vs. An Individual

According to Professor Kitayama and Professor Markus from University of Michigan, Asians and Westerners are different when introducing themselves.[3] Introducing oneself to others, either in formal or informal settings, is a common task for most people. However, how one presents oneself to others differs markedly by culture. Westerners introduce themselves by describing their personalities such them being kind, diligent, earnest, fun, or witty. They also describe their favorite activities. In contrast, Koreans, Chinese, and Japanese usually introduce themselves by describing their social status, role, membership to organizations and communities, and their current position.

Here's an example:

Westerner: I enjoy playing basketball with my friends and play other sports as well. I am also learning inline skating nowadays. I am a very cheerful and active person. I like Korean food too.

Asian: I am the eldest child in my family. I graduated from A University and I am currently working in the marketing department of A Electronics. I am an assistant manager at A Electronics. I was invited here today by Mr. Kim. Nice to meet you.

What differences did you observe? It may seem that the Asian introduction doesn't describe much about oneself. On the other hand, the Western introduction provides superficial, yet informative description of oneself such as personality, hobbies and favorites that provide a concise and clear picture of the person. Through their self-introductions, we can see a glimpse of how Asians and Westerners identify themselves.

"An angular stone gets chiseled." (equivalent to "Tall trees catch much wind" in the West) or "Don't try to stand out" are common Asian adages that show the Asian tendency to view individuality as detriment to the overall well-being of a society. For example, most people dress in monochromatic suits for professional occasions and generally refrain from accessorizing with color.

Asians identify themselves as a part of a family, community and society, and look to their relationships within these entities to seek their identities. In contrast, Westerners define themselves as an independent and free individual, allowing them to introduce themselves apart from their relationships.

B. Collectivism vs. Individualism

Because Asians value relationships with others and how others view themselves, Asian culture tends to focus on meeting the groups' expectations and maintaining good relations with its members. So when getting to know a person in Asian cultures, it is very important to know his or her job, peers, as well as which groups that person belongs to. Also it is important to note his or her position within the group. An Asian individual's identity is defined largely in part by one's relationships with others.

In Western societies, individual is the center of the universe. It is the fundamental, independent and most meaningful unit in society. Such culture is generally known to Asians as individualism. It is interesting to note that the word "individualism" does not exist in Asian cultures. In fact, such word does not exist in Chinese, Japanese, nor in Korean. Individualism in Asia has a slew of words such as "self-centered," "inconsiderate of others," "superficial," and "selfish." This is largely due to the fact that in Asia, historically agrarian, the value of cooperation in communities far outweighed individuality and independence.

Individualism is greatly valued in the West and consequently people from these individualistic societies pursue independent lives at a young age. Children are often raised in a separate bed and room from their parents and they learn the importance of not depending on others early on. Such practices are unimaginable in Asia. Asian children tend to be taken care of by their family, especially with their mothers, longer periods of time. Therefore, Western education provides children with the tools to lead independent lives, helping them develop self-confidence. This allows Westerners to exude confidence when sharing their strengths with others.

However, modesty is a virtue in collectivistic Asian societies. For instance, Asians generally display modesty by lowering themselves when speaking with others. Generally Asians view positively of those who share their opinions with others before reaching decisions, compared to those who are opinionated. This is because Asians are always aware of themselves as part of the group. We also see many Asian adages that praise modesty and humility about one's abilities and wisdom. "The boughs that bear most hang lowest" and "Empty vessels make the most sound" are Korean adages that illustrate the importance of modesty. Japanese also say "Most competent hawk hides its talons," which means that the talented do not parade their talent. These adages are opposite of Western norms. Moreover, the venerated Chinese scholar Laozi also writes in *Tao Te Ching*, "He who knows does not speak; he who speaks about it does not know it." While Westerners may fear that modesty would be disadvantageous, Asians trust that despite showing modesty and humility, others will acknowledge their abilities.

In collectivistic Asian societies that seek harmony, indirect communication is often used to avoid conflicts. On the other hand, Western societies that idealize individualism seek honest and direct communication. This will be covered in detail in Chapter 5.

C. Outsider's Perspective vs. Insider's Perspective

During lunch breaks, most Westerners order their dish of choice. Curiously, Asians are not like Westerners in these types of circumstances. Observe the following scenario.

When four out of the five coworkers on lunch break choose the same dish from a menu, or when a superior suggests a dish, how would you respond? Asians, especially Koreans, would choose the same dish as the other coworkers or follow the superior's suggestions. Why? According to Professor Cohen of University of Illinois, Westerners have an insider's perspective while Asians have an outsider's perspective.[4] With insider's perspective, the observer views the world from inside out, while with the outsider's perspective, the observer views the world from outside in. Westerners, who typically view the world inside out, tend to exhibit more self-centered tendencies than Asians, who typically view the world outside in. Those with insider's perspective focus on their own thoughts and emotions and believe that others behave similarly. Because Western cultures foster seeking and achieving one's own goals, it focuses on individual's thoughts and emotions that lead to different behavior.

In contrast, Asians have outsider's perspective, so they are more attuned to others' thoughts and emotions. While Asians do value their own thoughts and emotions, they also consider their relationship with others when deciding. In a culture that values cooperation and harmony, Asians emphasize the ability to take into account various circumstances and objectively evaluate oneself through the eyes of others. Therefore Asians are more accustomed to imagining oneself through the eyes of others.

Such differences are also translated into how individuals emotionally react to wrongdoings. Westerners often feel guilt when they commit something wrong. Because their worldview revolves around themselves, the emotional consequences from wrongdoings are directed towards themselves. Conversely, Asians feel shame because they view the world through relationships and communities. They feel others' reproach and contempt.

One of the most noticeable manifestations of the outsiders' perspective in Asia is the culture of "saving face," which we briefly mentioned in Chapter 1. Let us see how it relates to outsiders' perspective.

In Korea, saving face is defined by "other's opinion and others view" but in the context of this chapter, saving face can be understood as "displaying status-related behavior out of consciousness of status and thereby securing one's existence in the society" or "untruthful behavior depending on circumstance and relationship to increase one's (or other's) status."

Saving face applies not only to individual levels but also to family or national level. The society at large expends great energy on saving face and is sensitive to formalities. Specifically, Koreans are quite sensitive to size of objects. They tend to prefer large houses, cars and furniture. Regardless of how busy it is, large university hospitals receive more patients and large department stores attract more consumers despite their prohibitive prices.

Saving face is also part of sales in Asia. Sales people often say "Everyone is doing or buying this," to appeal to the consumers' need to save face. Moreover, they refer to the consumers using respected social positions such as "Mr. President," "Mrs. President," or "Teacher," regardless of their actual occupations.

Because Asians are always concerned with how others view them, they can sometimes feel uncomfortable when Westerners speak or behave in self-centered ways. For Westerners, saving face could be understood as trying to remain dignified in a given situation.

D. Situation vs. Human Nature

What would Westerners and Asians view as the cause of the following case?

Professor Morris and Professor Peng investigated the different perspectives of the US and China on a shooting incident at Iowa State University in 1991.[5] In 1991, a Chinese Ph.D student Lu Gang shot his advisor and wounded many others. Interestingly, the Eastern and Western media coverage on the same incident differed greatly. In the Western media, it was reported that the shooting took place because the Chinese student had personality and mental health issues. That is, the student murdered his colleagues because of psychological issues. For example, they reported that Lu Gang "had personality flaws," "had evil instincts," "believed firearms were best for revenge," "was dark and obsessed over success," and "could not stand others challenging him." However, the Asian media reported that the shooting took place because of Lu Gang's circumstances. The fact that he did not get along with his advisor and he failed to receive a degree was noted as contributing factors to the shooting incident.

To find out how differently they view this incident, Asians and Westerners were asked "Had Lu Gang found a job, would he have murdered his colleagues?" Westerners replied that he would have murdered his colleagues regardless of a job while Asians replied that he would not have done so.

Here, Professor Morris and Peng points out that Westerners think an individual's fundamental attribute caused the shooting. They also believe that these attributes do not change situationally but are fundamental to each individual. Westerners tend to focus on individual's attributes while Asians tend to focus on the background and the circumstances of the individual.[6]

E. High Context vs. Low Context

Culture anthropologist Edward Hall discusses the differences between high context and low context cultures in his book, *Beyond Culture.*[7] Low context cultures are direct and succinct in their communication and they communicate ideas clearly with both spoken and written words. High context cultures are indirect and vague. Their languages are implicit and considerate of the relationships between the speakers. Cultures that rely more on spoken or written words are low context while those that rely less on explicit expression are high context. Hall's conception of low versus high context can be viewed as part of our consideration of differences between the East and the West.

Western cultures are centered on humans. That is, it is focused on the object itself. Western cultures explore the nature and the properties of objects, and similarly explore the society at large. They seek generalizable logics and those that fit these logics become reasonable. On the other hand, Asian cultures are centered on relationships. Rather than having generally accepted social norms, each situation and context has its own appropriate norms that become the reasonable standard at the moment.

Put simply, high context cultures emphasize situations while low context cultures do not. To understand the main message in a high context culture's communication, one must pay more attention to the situation rather than the given message itself. Koreans, as well as Chinese and Japanese, are very sensitive to the "atmosphere," "sensation," "feelings" and require the communicators to understand them as well as the actual conversations and text. For example, phrases such as "add salt to taste," and "get a feel for the situation," are often very hard for Westerners to interpret because they are all very contextual in their nature. Westerners sometimes complain that they cannot know what Asians are thinking and this is likely because Asians speak indirectly.

Here is an example of an indirect statement of a parent when their child visits them: "Why are you here when you are so busy? You shouldn't have come!" No Asian child will take this statement literally and not visit their parents. Here is another indirect statement: "Go say hello to the client!" No Asian salesman literally will follow the superior's orders as it is and just say hello to the client.

Because Westerners believe that one must know the characteristics of an object to understand the object itself, they are not interested in contextual information. That is, they tend to focus on the given object and do not rely much on the physical or social environment, since they are in low context cultures.

Asian cultures are relatively homogenous and are based on Taoism, Confucianism and Buddhism, which praise silence, leading them to value context. Implicit, simple and abstract expressions became the norm in these societies. In contrast, in multicultural societies like the United States, specific expressions are necessary.

In Western societies that traditionally have trial by jury, the convicted must prove his or her innocence. In such instance, rhetoric and linguistic expressions would be very important, as one likely would not be able to prove innocence implicitly. Also, linguistic expressions become more efficient in multicultural societies with diverse populations. Typically, cultures with a long history of feudalism or authoritarian regimes tend to rely more on context while those with history of democracy tend to express their thoughts directly.

Because of these differences, it is natural for Asians to consider Westerners as being too direct or even rude. The two cultures differ greatly when writing letters and emails as well. Letters and emails written in high context cultures first ask the well-being of the recipient, explain how the writer is doing, and typically mention the main point of message briefly at the very end of the letter. On the other hand, letter and emails from low context cultures tend to mention the main point at the beginning.

This is why low context culture's logic is called linear logic while the high context culture's logic is called the spiral logic, because it touches on many different things to reach a conclusion at the end. In some cases, an Asian speaker may not actually conclude a conversation, but an Asian listener can easily draw the conclusion on their own. In contrast, low context cultures explicitly express their content so that the main message is usually at the very beginning of the conversation.

These contextual differences influence the different management styles of the East and the West. They are manifested in a variety of working relationships within an organization, such as communication, conflict management, feedback, and performance evaluation. These will be discussed in more detail in Chapters 5, 6, and 7.

F. Substance vs. Object

Let us take a look at the different conception of homogeneity for

Asians and Westerners, through Imai and Gentner's experiment.[8]

Here is a cylindrical object made of wood called "Dax." There are two other objects below the Dax. One is a blue plastic cylinder; the other is a wooden rectangular block. Which one of these objects is Dax?

Two cognitive psychologists, Mutsumi Imai and Dedre Gentner conducted this experiment on Asians and Westerners ranging from 2 year-old children to adults. Surprisingly, most Westerners selected the object with the same "shape" as Dax, while most Asians selected the one made of the same "material." This indicates that Asians consider the substance more important than the form while Westerners think vice versa.

For a clearer understanding, let us discuss the difference between Westerners' "object" versus the Asians' "substance." An object has a given volume, density, and shape. It is made of a given substance. For example, a desk, a chair, a nail and a pair of scissors, are objects. As such, an object refers to an entity with a specific shape, based on its external appearance regardless of its inner properties. This is closely tied with the Western perspective, which seeks stability, measurability and analyzability.

Substance is that which takes up space and has density. All objects are made of substances. Glass, wood, and steel are examples of substances. When focusing on size and appearance, we speak of objects and when focusing on the material that the object is consisted of, we speak of substances. For example, a ruler made of steel is an object and the steel is the substance. Substances can exist in many forms, but are generally in solid, liquid and gas form. This is closely tied with the Asian perspective which seeks changeability, mutability and the essence of the substance.

This study shows that Westerners and Asians see two different worlds. The applicable criteria for what is "similar" versus what is "different" can vary depending on whether the focus is on the substances from which objects are made of (such as wood versus plastic) or on the exterior form of the objects (such as round versus rectangular pillars). Depending on one's point of view, the concept of homogeneity can vary. If you look at an object as a "substance" point of view, the whole and parts are seen as one. If you look at an object in a "shape" point of view, the whole is a sum of parts.

Asians would agree that a "whole" is a single entity and it indicates a state of being complete while Westerners emphasize a "whole" is the sum of many individuals. Thus we see that Asians focus on the homogeneity and connection between the objects while Westerners analyze and distinguish by dissecting objects into smaller parts.

G. Relationship vs. Categorization

Categorization is the process of classifying concepts and objects by common properties and function for any given purpose. The purpose of categorization is ultimately a strategy to distinguish between the numerous concepts and objects to aid in understanding and remembering them. Ancient Chinese differed from Ancient Greeks on their categorization of the world in that they saw everything as being in "resonance" and belonging in one category.

We can further distinguish between the Western categorization where objects are classified by function and properties and the Asian categorization where objects are classified by relationships and cause-and-effect. Resonance, an Ancient Chinese idea, is what we call relationships today. According to the Ancient Chinese, a relationship is formed by cause and effect. As such, the Chinese put emphasis on the "resonance (relationship)" between objects while the Ancient Greeks categorized objects with common properties. For example, the Chinese believed that "spring, East, tree, wind, green" belong to the same category. This is because the change in the wind causes changes in the other four elements. However in Western cultures, spring would be categorized with summer, fall and winter and not with the East.

Through a simple experiment, Professors Ji, Zhang and Nisbett examined the different ways Asians and Westerners categorize objects.[9]

Cow	Chicken	Grass
Monkey	**Panda**	**Banana**
Magazine	**Notebook**	**Pencil**

- Which two objects would you group together in the first block?
- Which two objects would you group together in the second block?
- Which two objects would you group together in the third block?

Most Asians group cow and grass (cows feed on grass), monkey and banana (monkeys feed on bananas), and notebook and pencil (pencil is used to write on notebooks) together. Notice that the results are based on the relationships between the objects. On the other hand, Westerners tended to group cow and chicken (animals), monkey and panda (animals), and magazine and notebook (books) together. This reminds us of the Western categorization scheme. Based on scientific reasoning, cow and chicken are both mammals while the grass is not. Thus there is no apparent reason to classify cow and grass together.

Why, then, do Asians focus more on relationships when categorizing objects? The answer lies in the words "category" and "relationship." Categories are usually expressed in nouns while relationships in verbs. Going back to the previous example, we can see that cow and chicken, panda and monkey, and magazine and notebook are nouns. Nouns describe objects, entities, and matter. Thus, we can see that Westerners tend to categorize by nouns, which are distinguishable by its properties. In contrast, Asians categorize by describing the relationship between the two objects, such as "to eat" or "to use." While this difference may seem trivial, it is a crucial difference that resonates in how the two cultures differ in their viewpoints.

3 Cultural Differences in Everyday Life

A. Differences in Language Usage

Let us say you invited a friend to your house and the two of you are enjoying coffee together. How would you offer your friend to drink some more coffee?

Most Westerners would ask using nouns, such as "More coffee?" while Asians would ask using verbs, such as "Drink more?" In the individualistic West, a person and coffee are understood as independent entities and thus one uses the noun "coffee." Conversely, in the collectivistic East, a person and coffee is considered to have an interactive relationship, therefore one uses the verb "drink" in the question.

B. Differences in Consideration for Others

Let us compare an Asian restaurant versus a Western restaurant. When one eats at a Western restaurant, bread, salad, and meat are often served as a whole. This allows each person to cut their food to their liking with their own forks and knives. Such fork-and-knife culture allows diners to exercise choice, as they can select their own menu and serve themselves in their preferred size and amount.

On the other hand, Asian dishes are often served cut into bite size. Therefore, diners often only need chopsticks. Such chopstick-culture indicates the considerate nature of the Asians, as dishes are prepared with consideration of diners' comfort. However, this chopstick culture does not allow individuals to decide on the size of each bite.

Here's another example. When offering coffee to a guest, Asians and Westerners behave differently. When Asians offer coffee to a guest, cream or sugar is often added without asking. Although this has been slowly changing recently, it is not surprising to be served coffee with cream and sugar in Asia. However, Westerners may find this puzzling.

Instant coffee mixes (individually packed instant coffee with cream and sugar), which account for 25 percent of the Korean coffee market, have created its own niche through differentiating itself from instant coffee and brewed coffee. Apart from the convenience factor and the increased availability of water coolers that enabled the growth of the market, it is a brilliant product that was marketed on this peculiar aspect of Asian culture.

C. Differences in Taking Photographs

The East and the West differ even in taking photographs. With the expansion of the DSLR camera market, coupled with the growth of social networking services like Facebook, Twitter, and Flickr, we are constantly exposed to photographs.

In a simple experiment, Professor Masuda from University of Alberta asked both Western and Asian college students to take photographs of their friends.[10] He found that most Western students' photographs filled the entire frame with their friends while Asian students' photographs were usually wider-angled and included a fair amount of the background with their friends. From this experiment, we can infer that Asians take photographs to remember the location of a certain place at a certain time while Westerns take photographs to focus on the individual appearance, like facial expressions and attire.

4 Acknowledging and Understanding the Different Mindsets

If you are an Asian, you may feel that the eastern view is better and if you are a Westerner you may feel that the Western view is better. However, deeming only one side to be correct could provoke conflict between different ethnic groups. We need to remind ourselves that in today's rapidly globalizing world, there are many exchanges between Eastern and Western countries thus diverse ethnic groups and citizens must learn to live harmoniously. We should acknowledge and understand the diversity of the Eastern and Western mindsets. Lastly, we should also realize that the differences between the East and the West can help moderate the respective errors generated by each side because each culture is right and justifiable for its own people.

2

Comparing South Korea, China, and Japan

You may have felt from the previous section that not all "Western" countries share the same patterns of behavior and mindset, nor do all Asian countries share the same behaviors and mindset. It should be noted that our comparisons only serve to highlight the major differences.

Let us take a closer look at Korea, China and Japan. Many people are familiar with China and Japan but relatively less so with Korea. Since Westerners tend to know more about China and Japan than Korea, the comparison of three nations will help you better understand Korea.

1 Exchanges amongst South Korea, China, and Japan

UN Member States – 194 countries

World Atlas – 237 countries

World Bank – 229 countries

Among the many countries neighboring one another, it would be hard to find neighbors so different as Korea, China and Japan. Even the UK, France and Germany, often dubbed as the most different countries, share some similarities. For example, they share similar religions, use the same alphabets, and use forks and knives as their utensils. However, these three Eastern countries could not be any more different.

When non-Asians think of Asia, they often think that Korea, China and Japan are very similar. They tend to think that since they look similar and share the influence of Chinese culture and Confucianism, all three countries must have similar cultures as well. However, these three countries each have unique cultures. While they share broad similarities in their general mindsets and behaviors, each differs in the values that they pursue and how problems are solved. This leads to significant differences in how each culture conducts business.

The three Far East countries exchanged with each other throughout history but their borders remained relatively unchanged, as well did the direction of cultural flow. Culture was first transferred from China to Korea and then Korea to Japan. Because these countries prohibited exchange between the people apart from diplomatic and trade relations, each country has maintained a relatively distinct history and culture. However, it should be noted that all three countries share a strong tie of being the "same race."

2 Language Differences

Many European countries speak Romance languages. Since they share the same Latin root in their languages, most Europeans are able to communicate with each other on a basic level despite the language differences. Some European countries have multiple, official languages and many Europeans are multilingual. However, although Korea, China and Japan are neighboring countries that share common linguistic roots from Chinese characters, their languages are so far apart that they cannot converse without interpreters.

Mainland Chinese use simplified Chinese characters while the Japanese use their own characters called *Kana*. Koreans use *Hangul*, a unique alphabet system that was invented approximately 570 years ago. *Hangul* is widely acknowledged to be the most scientifically designed alphabet in the world for several reasons: the shapes of many of the consonants are graphical representations of the speech organs used to pronounce them, it can express more sounds than any other existing alphabet system, and it is the easiest alphabet to learn and use.

3 Differences Based on Geographical Location

Korea is located between China and Japan. All three countries are all located in the Far East. However, the three countries have distinctly different geopolitical characteristic. China is a continental state, Korea is a peninsula state, and Japan is an island state. These geopolitical differences are reflected in the culture of each country. First, we provide a factual overview about the three countries.

A. Korea

Korea is a peninsula state. Peninsular cultures tend to pursue independence and protect their traditions. The fact that the Balkan countries fight to maintain their ethnicities despite foreign invasions and the diverse population serves as a testament to this characteristic.

People from peninsular states often hold onto their exclusivity by refusing to assimilate with other ethnicities and fighting to maintain their traditions. This results in a unique sense of pride that serves as a basis in their temperamental, stubborn and uncompromising disposition.

A peninsula state is stable when it is strong but becomes an easy target for its neighboring countries when its powers wane. This is because peninsulas are gateways into continents and become a convenient hub to expand from within the continent. For China and Russia the Korean Peninsula is a strategic hub for their overseas expansion while for Japan, it is a necessary gateway into the Asian continent. This inevitably caused Korea to suffer many foreign invasions from these countries over the years. Historically, Korea is known to have been attacked over 900 times since the country was established.

Because war has been a constant threat in peninsular states, its people tend to focus on survival. The need to protect their own family's lives and wealth enabled them to foster a keen sense of unity based on kinship. However, without threat, they behave surprisingly individualistic with little room for negotiation. They often exhibit small-scale collectivism, a mixture of collectivism and individualism; they tend to be more collectivist or more individualistic depending on the issue at hand. For example, when the state becomes the focal group that becomes salient in people's minds, they become tremendously patriotic in order to preserve the country's independence. Similarly, when a company becomes the focal group, they concentrate on working for the company's profits as a common goal. Therefore, leadership in Korea is based on how to conceptualize its group as a family-like unit to activate their sense of unity.

B. China

China is a continental state. China's continental characteristics are manifested in the idea that it is the center of the world. The Chinese characters for the word "China" mean "the Middle Kingdom." For centuries, the Chinese have had a sense of pride that their country is the center of the world and the center of civilization. Like China, the people of continental France also believe that France is the best country and the best ethnic group based on its rich history and culture. Furthermore, just as France took in other ethnic groups' culture with the virtue of tolerance, China was able to embrace brief foreign rule by the Mongolians and the Manchurians as part of a unique Chinese culture.

People in the continental states exhibit marked individuality. Regardless of who governs a nation, their own happiness and safety should always come first. The Chinese also are not too concerned about who their king is or what form of government is established; they consider the individual to be the most important.

Since China was a sprawling nation that made centralized rule very difficult, they paid little attention to its small neighboring countries and remained at peace as long as they didn't pose a direct threat. However, sometimes the "China is the center of the world" attitude lent itself to violent attempts by the military to conquer its neighboring countries. Unfortunately, China continues to try to overpower its neighbors with force; its conflict with Uigur and Tibet are good example of such instances. Also, China is very adept at politics of power, as it showed in the recent incident in the Senkaku Islands, sometimes referred to as the Pinnacle Islands. While Japan insisted on trial by Japanese law for the arrested Chinese sailors, China succeeded in obtaining the release of the sailors by threatening to block exports of industrial products to Japan. In similar fashion, China uses their supply of crude oil to North Korea as leverage when dealing with North Korea in international politics.

C. Japan

Japan is an island state. Island states often develop a unique subtlety and refinement in their culture since they suffer less foreign invasion with the sea as their protection. The island state countries consider harmony very important because their people must peacefully coexist in limited land. The idea that conflict can only lead to mutual destruction made them value harmony as a virtue. To facilitate this, these states often worship a single, godlike figure (in many cases, a monarch) who serves as a mediator in conflicts.

In island states, a single ruler rules and mediates in the early stages of a country's development. However, the structure of an island state often lends itself to a dual power structure. In Japan, the *Tenno* (Japanese emperor) is the symbol of the nation, while the actual political power is in the hands of a Prime Minister. The United Kingdom is another island state that has a similar dual structure where the monarch serves as a symbolic authority and the Prime Minister serves as the actual political leader.

Islanders try to avoid bumping heads with each other to prevent conflicts. To avoid interpersonal conflict, arguably the most dangerous event in an island state, islanders try to avoid aggressive behavior in their encounters with each other. Therefore, manners and consideration of others become the basis of social relationships in an island state.

There's a saying that highlights the Japanese concepts of "*honne*" and "*tatemae*." It is said that "The Japanese speak with two tongues." This means the Japanese have one tongue that speaks sweetly in front of others and another one that speak maliciously behind their backs. Of course, one must not generalize that all Japanese practice this but not showing their true *honne* and instead showing their *tatemae* is ingrained as part of their culture.

In June 1944, around the time that the US began its strike on Japan, Ruth Benedict was asked by the US Department of Defense to write a book to better understand Japan. In her book *Chrysanthemum and the Sword*, she writes, "When an author writes a book on a nation with a popular cult of aestheticism which gives high honor to actors and to artists and lavishes art upon the cultivation of chrysanthemums, that book does not ordinarily have to be supplemented by another which is devoted to the cult of the sword and the top prestige of the warrior. ··· The Japanese are to the highest degree aggressive and unaggressive, both militaristic and aesthetic, both insolent and polite, rigid and adaptable, submissive and resentful of being pushed around, loyal and treacherous, brave and timid, conservative and hospitable to new ways."[11]

Excluding two unsuccessful attacks by the Mongols in the 13th century and the US occupation post-World War II, Japan was never attacked in its entire history. Civil wars within Japan were not wars of conquest but power struggles between the power elites. However, when faced with foreign invasions, they unite strongly, prioritizing the needs of the group over that of the individual and giving utmost importance to the fulfillment of each individual's responsibility to the group.

Due to the xenophobia common in island nations, Japanese culture was influenced by foreign cultures more slowly than those of the continental states. When the Japanese find it necessary to accept another culture, they do so selectively, transforming it into their own. Japanese absorbed Chinese, Korean and Western culture since the 15th century and synthesized these influences into their own unique culture. Japan's culture developed into a delicate feminine culture rather than a masculine one. However, since people are restrained in their outward expressions of their emotions and are required to exercise tremendous self-restraint, these pent up emotions display themselves in often peculiar ways. Prevalence of perverse crimes in Japan and the notorious Hooligans of the UK are examples where such restrained emotions and energy are thought to be expressed.

4 Lifestyles Differences

Many Westerners regard Korea, China and Japan as having the same Chinese cultural influences and expect them to share similar lifestyles. It is true that there are many similarities between these countries. However, they also have their unique cultures and lifestyles. Therefore, if we can learn the differences in the three countries' lifestyles from this chapter, we will understand each country and its people better. Here, we highlight several key examples that will be helpful in learning the different lifestyles of Korea, China and Japan.

A. Comparing the Different Spoon and Chopstick Cultures

One of the similar yet different elements of these three countries' lifestyles is the way people use spoons and chopsticks to eat food. All three countries use spoons and chopsticks to eat; while Chinese and Japanese use spoons to eat soup, Koreans consider spoons to be somewhere between forks and chopsticks and use them to eat both soup and rice.

Korean chopsticks are thin and medium length, Chinese chopsticks are long and thick, and Japanese chopsticks are short and have pointy ends.

In Korea, chopsticks are used as a supplement for spoons and are used to pick up food. Koreans pick up side-dish foods, called *banchan*, piece by piece with their thin and heavy chopsticks. To pick up foods like anchovies or beans, delicate chopstick skills are required.

On the other hand, Chinese and Japanese use chopsticks to sweep food into their mouths. Chinese mostly hold chopsticks together and push their food to one side of the dish, put the dish to their mouths and push the food into their mouths with the chopsticks. Japanese also use chopsticks to put food directly into their mouths in similar fashion. The difference from the Korean way of using chopsticks is that while Koreans pick up food with their chopsticks, Japanese put the food in between the chopsticks.

B. Comparing Lifestyles

There are also other differences in the Korean, Chinese and Japanese lifestyle.

The Koreans and the Japanese generally lead a lifestyle that involves sitting on the floor. However, even though both have a sitting-on-the-floor lifestyle, Koreans prefer the *ondol* system that provides heat from stone under the floor while the Japanese use woven reed mats called *tatami* for their floors. Nowadays, neither the Koreans nor the Japanese insist on having only a floor seating culture. They use chairs and beds, and many families use a combination of the two styles. On the contrary, the Chinese use furnitures such as beds and chairs in everyday life, similar to Westerners.

Korea, China and Japan are different in their traditional costume as well. The Korean traditional costume, *hanbok*, was made to emphasize the wearer's face, so it is designed to cover body curvatures. However, many modernized *hanbok* are designed nowadays to showcase both the beauty of the *hanbok* itself and the beauty of the body. In traditional China, women bound feet so they couldn't run. The Chinese traditional dress, *chi pao*, is distinguished by its long slit along the side of the skirt that is indicative of the sexually liberal culture of China. The Japanese considered the chest area important as it symbolized the prosperity of the future generation. Therefore, the Japanese traditional costume, the *kimono*, protects the chest area with several layers of fabrics.

C. Comparing Religion

Korea became the most Confucius country of the three after the establishment of the *Joseon* Dynasty when Confucianism was promoted and Buddhism was suppressed. However, emancipation from the Japanese control brought the end of religious repression and Korea became a country with religious freedom. Today, about 22.8 percent of Koreans believe in Buddhism, 18.3 percent Protestantism, and 10.9 percent Catholicism.[12] China has been considered as the birthplace of Confucianism. However, Chinese beliefs are largely based on Taoism, which focuses on cherishing the individual's happiness and well-being. When Buddhism was brought to Japan, freedom of religion was proclaimed from the fear that there might be a conflict between Buddhism and Shintoism, Japan's traditional religion.

As such, although Korea, China and Japan are in the same East Asian ethnic group with similar appearances, they show various differences when it comes to language, geographical location, and lifestyle. As mentioned, knowing the differences among these three countries will be valuable knowledge when meeting Koreans, Chinese and Japanese.

Summary of Chapter 2

1. Differences between Asian and Western Ways of Thinking

- Asians identify themselves as a part of a family, community and society. They look to their relationships within these entities to seek their identities. In contrast, Westerners identify themselves as an independent and free individual.
- An Asian individual's identity is defined largely in part by one's relationships with others. In Western societies, the individual is the center of the universe. The individual is the fundamental, independent and most meaningful unit in society.
- Asians understand another person's thoughts or emotions by considering their own emotions and the relationship they have with the other person. Westerners focus on their own thoughts and emotions and tend to believe that others think and feel the same way as they do.
- Western cultures are centered on humans. It is focused on the object itself. On the other hand, Asian cultures are centered on relationships. Rather than having generally accepted social norms, each situation and context has its own appropriate norms that become the reasonable standard.
- Asians would agree that a "whole" is a single entity and indicates a state of being complete while Westerners emphasize the individuality of things, viewing the "whole" as the sum of many individuals. Thus we see that Asians focus on the homogeneity and the connection between objects while Westerners analyze and distinguish by dissecting objects into smaller parts.
- The Ancient Chinese differed from the Ancient Greeks in their categorization of the world. Ancient Chinese thought everything in the same "resonance" belonged in one category. As such, the Chinese put emphasis on the "resonance (relationship)" between objects while the Ancient Greeks categorized objects with common properties.

2. Comparing South Korea, China, and Japan

- Korea is located in between China and Japan. All three countries are located in the Far East. However, geopolitically, they have different characteristics. China is a continental state, Korea is a peninsula state and Japan is an island state.
- Korea, China and Japan share many similarities, however they each have a distinct culture, language and lifestyles.

Chapter 03

The Social System of Korea

In this chapter, we will study Korea's social system by looking at the Korean way of thinking and lifestyle. By the end of this chapter that covers the age, family, education, language, clothing, food, and housing of Koreans, you will be able to comprehend their way of communication.

First, let us look at the conversation between a Korean family and a visiting foreigner.

Skit

In front of the traditional Korean house's entrance

Mrs. Kim: Hello. Welcome.

Foreigner: Is this Mr. Kim's residence?

Mrs. Kim: Yes. We were expecting you.

Door opens with a squeak, sequentially shows painting, eaves, roof, and floor

Mr. Kim: Welcome, Chuck. Did you have any difficulties finding the house?

Figure 3-1 *Hanok*

Figure 3-2 *Danchong*

Foreigner: Not at all. Your directions were easy to follow.

Mr. Kim: Please come on in. Would you like a quick tour of the house? The house is built in the traditional Korean house style called *hanok*. Would you like to explain, dear?

Mrs. Kim: Of course, I would love to. Chuck, is this your first time visiting a traditional Korean house? Please come this way.

(stands up and walks towards the eaves, pointing at the painting on the edge of the roof) We call that "*Danchong*."

Isn't it colorful? Those paintings are there not only as decoration, but also as a protection for the house from erosion caused by rain and wind.

(pointing at the eaves) Look at the eaves. We call them "*Cheoma*."

In a traditional Korean house, the eaves show the beauty of the entire roof and its curves. In addition to its elegance, it protects and preserves the structure and controls the temperature inside.

Foreigner: Wow, the curves on the roof are just beautiful. The eaves and color of the painting are magnificent. (sitting on the wooden floor)

Mr. Kim: Now, shall we sit and have a cup of tea?

Figure 3-3 *Cheoma*

Foreigner: Thank you.

Mr. Kim and the foreigner enjoying conversation and smiling

In Korean culture, the host serves tea first and treats his/her guest to the best hospitality when visiting his/her home.

Let us take a look at a traditional Korean house. *Hanok* is different from a contemporary house. Central to the *hanok* is the main living room, surrounded by other rooms. The kitchen and bathroom are either accessed by passing through the main living room or are located in separate buildings. Materials such as wood, mud, and hay are used in *hanok*. The basic layout of *hanok* consists of the main interior, guest area, shrine, servants' quarters, a separate house, and storage. The main interior, located furthest away from the main gate, is where the ladies of the household stay. It usually consists of a main bedroom, living room, second room, and the kitchen. The guest area is where the guests of the house stay. It is also used for entertaining relatives and guests, or used as a study.

skit

suddenly, the foreigner's stomach growls

Mr. Kim: Well, you must be hungry. Let's have dinner.

from the table in the kitchen, Mrs. Kim enters wearing the traditional Korean clothing, hanbok

Mr. Kim: Now, let's have a seat.

Mrs. Kim: Chuck, I wanted to show you the traditional Korean attire, so I wore my *hanbok*. What do you think?

Foreigner: Wow, that is very elegant and pretty. It really is beautiful!

Men's *hanbok* includes pants and a top, and women's *hanbok* includes a skirt and a top. When dressing for an occasion, an outer garment called "*Durumagi*" is worn.

skit

table with food laid out

Mrs. Kim: Chuck, please help yourself.

Mr. Kim: I hope you enjoy it.

Foreigner: Thank you. (fumbling with chopsticks. To himself: Hmmm...using chopsticks is harder than I thought.)

Mr. Kim and Mrs. Kim are sharing one dish with chopsticks and the spoons.

Foreigner: (To himself: This seems a little unhygienic. It doesn't seem very appealing.)

As Chuck finishes eating, the wife urges him to have more food.

Mrs. Kim: Please have some more.

Foreigner: I have had enough. Thank you.

Figure 3-4 Korean table setting

Koreans place all of their dishes in the center of the table and enjoy them at the same time. There is no concept of main and side dishes in Korea. Several assorted side dishes are also shared by everyone. It is not easy to use chopsticks for the first time. Korean chopsticks are especially difficult to use because they are thin and heavy. Getting used to using chopsticks generally takes about a week.

Korea has a culture of sharing food together. However, since many foreigners are not used to this, restaurants often serve individual portions in separate dishes or provide separate chopsticks to be used as serving utensils. As in many other cultures, Koreans want their house guests to eat a lot. Since food was very scarce in the past, serving generously was considered good hospitality and guests in return showed their respect by eating a lot of food.

Skit

Mr. Kim's oldest son comes in to say hello.

Mrs. Kim: Excuse me, Chuck, how old are you? Are you married?

Foreigner: (a little flustered) Uh . . . Yes. . . .

Mrs. Kim: Minsoo, say hello to Chuck.

Mr. Kim's son: (bowing head to say hello) How do you do, sir?

Foreigner: Hello, how are you? Nice to meet you.

Mrs. Kim: How many children do you have, Chuck?

Foreigner: (To himself: She is asking too many private questions in a first meeting) Eh? Oh... two.

Saying good-bye when leaving the house.

Foreigner: Whew, although it was an enjoyable evening, there were many bewildering moments as well.

As we can see, when Koreans meet someone for the first time, they are mostly interested in the other's personal information. This is Koreans' way of engaging in a conversation with another person in a proper manner. We will explore this more in detail later.

Discovering new cultures is enjoyable, but also difficult at the same time. Knowing the Korean social system before coming to Korea or meeting Koreans will help you understand their culture more easily and prevent frustration and confusion. Every country has a uniquely different culture and one should not try to judge whether each difference is good or bad. Understanding and accepting each other's cultural differences is the first step in communication and preparation for successful business.

1

Age

Did you notice how Mrs. Kim asked Chuck's age at the initial meeting? That's how important age is to Koreans. In Korean culture, how you treat a person can vary widely depending on that person's age. Let us now examine how central age is to Korean culture and how that affects both the daily lives and the business dealings of Koreans.

While asking someone's age can be considered very rude in many countries, it is very important to Koreans even in business dealings because of Korean language's honorific grammar and determining hierarchy. When you meet Koreans, you will realize immediately that they are very interested in your age whether in business or social settings.

1 Age Is the Fairest Standard

The Korean way of counting age is a little different than in the West. When a Korean person says his age, he might say "I am 32 years old according to the Korean way of counting age, and 31 years old according to the Western way."

Now, let us look at how Koreans count their age. Koreans calculate their age from the moment of birth. In the Western world, a newborn is 0 years old, but Koreans consider a newborn as one year old. This is because the fetus is considered to be a person from the moment of conception. Why do Koreans think this way? To Koreans, babies have always been viewed as a life given by the gods, rather than being created by a human couple. Thus, even an unborn child in the womb is considered a person in Korea. Of course, this idea is not consistent with modern science.

Doesn't this also happen in the Western world? Here is a famous anecdote. A pregnant lady was driving "alone" in the carpool lane and was given a ticket by a police officer. This lady stated in front of a judge, "I was not alone. There were two of us: me and the baby in my belly." The judge accepted this statement and said the fine did not have to be paid. Anti-abortion movements in the West also view fetuses as people.

Because Koreans believe heaven bestows their babies, couples unable to have children often visit temples or churches to pray, or climb mountains to plea to the gods. Because age is something that humans cannot control, Koreans view it as being the fairest standard for determining one's rank in society.

Koreans consider age to be a very important factor in deciding whether to show someone respect. In Korea showing respect to the elderly is considered a common courtesy. Does this mean the birth order is the most important thing in Korean society? It is, only when there is no other information available.

Koreans think that "All people are created equally by the god." This ideal is essential in Korean culture and customs. However, because Koreans stress relationships between individuals, it is important to establish order between people. Even though everyone is considered equal, it is very important to establish each other's position in a hierarchy, whether in an organization or in day-to-day living.

It is not easy to determine hierarchy based on superficial standards (e.g. education, wealth, occupation) when you first meet a stranger. Koreans believe that age is the easiest and the fairest standard for establishing order. As mentioned before, a person's birth is not something controlled by humans but rather a higher being's will; consequently it is the fairest benchmark.

Asking one's age may be considered as an invasion of privacy, but it is conventionally exchanged to set the manners and etiquette within the group for Koreans. When one does not prefer to disclose exact age, he/she can provide information such as high school or undergraduate graduation year or the age of his/her first child to let others estimate.

"The order in which teeth come out," is an old Korean saying that demonstrates that for Koreans, determining hierarchy based on birth date is the fairest. Even today, authority within Korean organizations is most often determined by seniority. Of course, this is less likely nowadays as more and more organizations shift towards meritocracy but there is no denying that seniority still exists. We will discuss more about equality and seniority in a later chapter.

Now, shall we ask an intriguing question here? What happens if Koreans get into a car accident and argument arises between the two drivers? What would be the first thing they say? When conflict arises between Koreans, they ask each other's age to determine seniority. The person who asks "How old are you?" first is usually the older one. This stems from the desire to be in a superior position before trying to resolve the dispute. Foreigners often do not understand why determining seniority has anything to do with trying to establish who was at fault.

2 Korean Honorifics, Honorific Rules

The reason why age is so important is because it is related to honorifics, an aspect of Korean language that foreigners find the hardest to learn. Honorifics and its ever-complex rules on titles and sentence structure differ greatly depending on the relative seniority of the people involved in a conversation. Therefore, knowing people's relative seniority is a very important matter of etiquette to address people politely. More than anything else, this is why Koreans want to know each other's age at first encounter.

3 The Way to Ask Someone's Age

Now, can you see why Koreans consider age to be so important in personal relationships? The first thing Koreans wonder when they meet strangers or meet a foreigner is how old he/she is. As shown in an intriguing question above, they feel superior to or expect respect from younger people.

In most countries, asking someone's age directly may be rude. However, Koreans will try to find out the person's age through indirect means because of its importance in forming relationships. They will try to get a feel for someone's age by asking the indirect questions such as, "When did you start college?", "When did you graduate from college?", "How many years have you worked at your company?" or "How old is your child?" and hope to estimate the person's age from that information.

When Koreans cannot determine someone's age, they will likely feel very uncomfortable because they do not know how to behave or speak properly. This concept of honorifics is rooted in Koreans' subconscious and often becomes a source of confusion when they speak English.

4 Practical Application Tip

A typical situation when seniority becomes an issue in an organizational setting is when a superior in an organization is younger than his or her subordinates. In most cases this does not pose a problem in a work environment. However, this could potentially lead to a disastrous outcome in dispute. When disputes arise between a younger superior and an older subordinate, it is best to remain polite and respectful for both parties. To openly criticize or command with disrespect will lead to further escalation of unnecessary tension. A wiser alternative would be to privately engage in a conversation and resolve the dispute by asking clarifying questions or advice. Asking for advice signals to the senior subordinate that the younger superior acknowledges their seniority and experience, therefore allowing the senior subordinate to feel respected and save face.

Confirming What You've Learned

Your colleague, Thomas, works with an older Korean, Mr. Lee. One day Thomas is arguing with Mr. Lee about a job that was not handled properly. Suddenly Mr. Lee yells, "How old are you? How dare you act this way!" and leaves. Other Koreans in the area tell Thomas that he went too far. Thomas says he only brought up issues that had merit and cannot understand why Koreans get so emotional over a trivial issue. What kind of advice would you give to Thomas?

Expert Opinion In Korean society that endorses an age-based hierarchy, age is a very important factor when dealing with another person. Of course, within an organization, position and duties take precedence over age. However, this does not mean you can completely disregard the age factor. When a subordinate or fellow worker is older than you, considering their age and using honorifics accordingly is considered courteous when speaking to a Korean. Even when conflicts arise at work, using honorifics when speaking to senior fellow coworkers is important.

Koreans do not like open conflicts or arguments, especially in front of others. There is always a chance that Mr. Lee felt that Thomas started an argument which was rooted in personal issues, rather than work-related issues. If such a conflict arises within an organization, trying to resolve it in front of others is not appropriate. Rather, efforts should be made to use indirect methods or to have only those directly involved in the problem meet discreetly and resolve it in private.

2 Family

To understand Koreans, we need to learn about how Koreans regard family and understand the different roles of each member in the family.

1 The Meaning of Family to Koreans

First, let us study the Korean family life cycle. The chart below illustrates the typical life cycle of a Korean family.

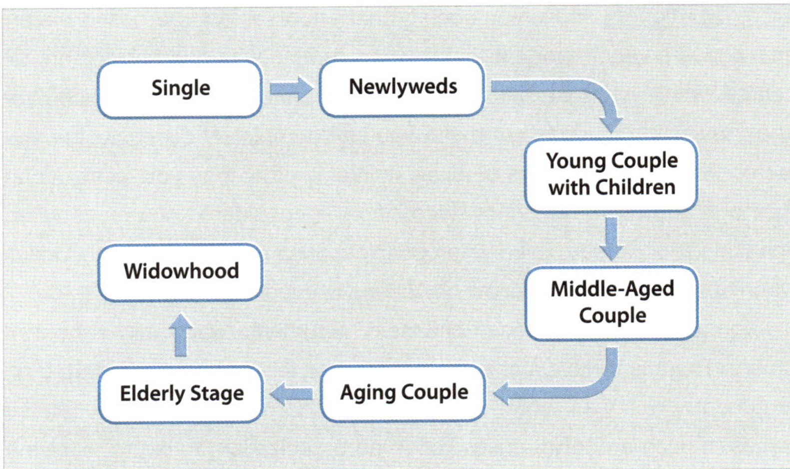

Figure 3-5 A typical Korean family life cycle

The most interesting point here is that unlike in the West where going to college usually marks the beginning of independence for a child, Korean children generally live at home with their parents until they get married. In many cases, children will live with their parents even past thirty, unless in special circumstances such as when they have a long commute to work. Traditionally, Korea has an extended family system where the grandparents live together with their eldest or the firstborn son and his family. Over time, family size has become much smaller in Korea, but it is still perceived as a social norm today for the eldest son or the firstborn child to take care of his or her parents.

A. Single

Generally, it is normal for unmarried children to live with their parents. However, some children live independently from their parents due to a long commute to work or other special circumstances.

B. Newlyweds

Before a newly married couple has their first child, life revolves around the couple.

C. Young Couple with Children

This is the period after the birth of a child, but before the child begins elementary school. It is at this stage that the living pattern shifts from revolving around the couple to revolving around the child. Koreans are deeply affectionate toward their children and therefore Korean family life centers around the children.

D. Middle-Aged Couple

During this period, children attend school and family life revolves around their education and family recreation.

E. Aging Couple

This is the period after the children finish schooling and enter the workforce. In Korea, children often receive financial support from their parents when they get married.

F. Elderly Stage

This is the stage when all children are independent and the parents are alone again. Family life once again revolves around the couple and they enjoy a more financially stable life than that of newlyweds. Of course, there are still many parents who live with their children at this stage.

G. Widowhood

In Korea, a widowed parent usually lives with his or her children. Although in the past the firstborn son usually took care of the parent, nowadays it is more likely that any child who is affordable takes care of their parent.

Regardless of nationality and ethnicity, family and their happiness are important to everyone. However, the definition of a family's happiness and how the family expresses love for one another differs slightly between Koreans and foreigners.

For Westerners, it is important that life revolves around the family and spends a lot of time together as a family. Koreans also love their families and view them importantly, but they believe that each family member has a unique role to play in the family and playing that role to the best of their abilities is ultimately what is best for the family.

Of course Koreans and Westerners both love their families, but there is a difference in how they seek happiness for their family. The main role of men in Korea is to earn a living to support the family by working very long hours. This may appear to Westerners as if Koreans consider work more important than family. The main role of women in Korea is to handle the children's education and the family's finances. Historically in Korea, women held the keys to where the family riches were stored in each household.

However, for the younger generation, such roles are becoming Westernized. For example, both men and women separately manage one's finances than as a family and they share household chores. Still, many wives are in charge of managing family finances and often invest in real estate to grow their family assets.

Recently, an increasing number of women with higher education encouraged and allowed for more women to participate in economic activities in Korea. However, according to a recent study on the social status of women, Korean women still only ranked in the middle range relative to the rest of the world. In 2010, the Economist Intelligence Unit, a British group that compiles economic data, rated the social standing and position of women in 113 countries around the world. Korea scored 78.3 out of 100, which placed it in the 66th place among all the countries rated.

Although there clearly needs to be greater efforts in raising the social status of Korean women, we would like to look at this matter from a different angle. From the standpoint of the democratic and Christian values of the Western world, it may seem that Korean women have very low social status, while in Scandinavian countries, especially in Sweden, women's status seem to be very high. However, this is largely dependent on how one defines "power of women." If it is defined as social success, savings, open marriage, and freedom from the pressures of family life, Sweden can very well seem like a paradise for women. Conversely, if it is defined by how much they are involved in household decision-making processes, one could say that Korean women have higher social status.

In Korea, women make nearly all of the decisions on important matters including household finances, children's education, and buying a home. Since long ago, it was women's duty to be in charge of the keys to household storage and it was men's duty to earn a living. While the financial administration of the household was a woman's duty, such structured roles have been slowly changing with the younger generation. Younger couples these days seem to be more westernized with each having their own bank accounts while sharing household duties. However, the accumulation of wealth still seems to be the duty of the wife and real estate investments seem to be the most widely used means of accumulating and storing wealth in Korea.

2 Koreans' Views on Country and Family

Which is more important to Koreans, their own country or family? Based on the Korean value system, family is more important than their own country. In Korea, family tradition comes before all else. Even today, corporations generously excuse their employees from work to tend to their family matters. The same applies to schools, where students can make up their exams when they coincide with major family occasions such as weddings and funerals.

The idea that family is more important than country can be seen in the Korean traditional custom which honors one's parents for three years after their passing. Long ago, when a parent passed away, the surviving children built a small hut near the grave and spent three years there while remembering the wishes of their parents. During this time, they wore rough clothes and ate coarse food while living in the hut.

Why did they do this for three years? This comes from an ancient Chinese idea that a child cannot survive without the care of his parents for at least three years after being born, so the parents were looked after for same amount of time after their death.

During the *Joseon* Era, there was a general whose father had recently passed away. When he protested that he could not fight in the war because he had not taken care of his father for the full three years after his death, the King excused him from his military duties. We can clearly see here how important family is to Koreans.

3 Korean Appellation

Koreans often use family related terms to speak to or address strangers as a way of showing their consideration for all members of society. By examining the way Koreans address one another, we can learn about their mentality towards family and the community.

In order to convey closeness or show consideration, Koreans will call non-family-members, even strangers, "auntie" and "grandma" or "uncle" and "grandpa." Koreans will refer to a middle-aged woman as *ajumma*, which literally means aunt. A middle-aged man is called *ajeossi*, or uncle. Older women are referred to as *halmeoni*, a grandmother, and an older man is referred to as *halabeoji*, a grandfather. Originally the terms *ajumma* and *ajeossi* were used for older relatives. *Ajumma* meant female relatives, and *ajeossi* meant male adult relatives. *Halmeoni* and *halabeoji* are only supposed to be used for one's grandmother or grandfather, but use of these terms has expanded to also include elderly people with whom one has no family relations. The use of such terms conveys a desire to develop an affectionate, family-like relationship with the person and allows them to feel closer. For Koreans, the concept of family extends to the community as well. Additionally, the designation "you" is only used for someone of similar age or younger.

Westerners do not extend the concept of family to the community. To express fondness, one can use names in a personable and friendly way, or address people using titles such as "Sir," "Ma'am" or "Madam." Unlike Koreans, Westerners would not refer to the female owner of a restaurant they frequent as "aunt."

Take a look at this kinship chart. Koreans maintain family relations with even very distant relatives. In the past, those with the same last names from the same family branch were forbidden by law to marry, but now only marriages between distant third cousins are prohibited. In Korea, family relationships are distinguished by the number of "*Chon*," which helps show the degree one person is related to another. Couples are designated as being zero "*Chon*" and parent-child relationships are defined as one "*Chon*." The number of "*Chon*" used indicates family relationships and expresses the closeness of the family tie. If the "*Chon*" number is high, the relatives will most likely not know each other. These days, most families keep in touch with relatives within about six "*Chon*."

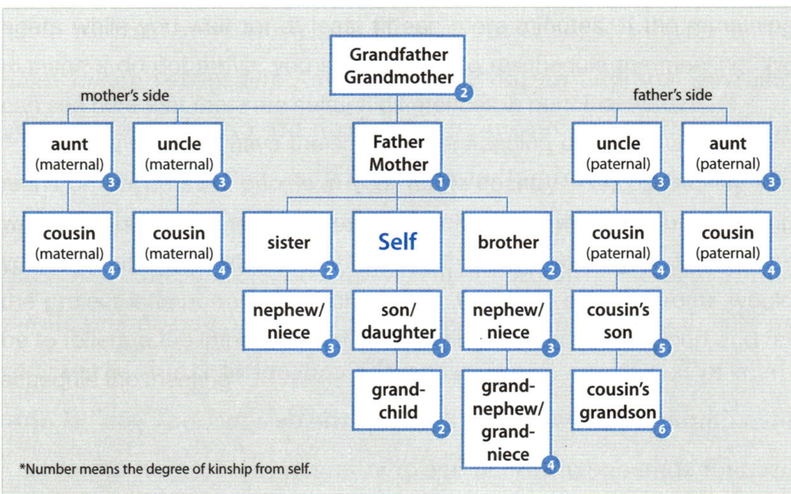

Figure 3-6 Kinship chart

Getting all of these relatives together in one place is very difficult, but most get together for Korean holidays. Koreans gather together for New Year's Day, the Korean harvest festival day, *Chuseok*, and for commemoration and honor passed away parents by visiting their graves. Because of this, during certain holidays, millions of people visit their families, causing huge traffic jams on major highways. This is another example highlighting the importance of family for Koreans.

Korean Holidays

Lunar New Year's (*Seolnal*)

Lunar Year's is celebrated at the beginning of each year based on the lunar calendar and is considered one of the biggest Korean holidays. At the start of the Lunar New Year, it is customary to dress in traditional Korean clothing and visit one's family.

Chuseok

This holiday celebrated on August 15th of the lunar calendar is called the *Chuseok*. This takes place during the harvest season when food is abundant. It is a time to thank the ancestors and visit relatives to share happiness and give thanks. It is a holiday much like the Thanksgiving Day in America.

Jesa

Jesa is a memorial service to honor one's deceased parents and ancestors by offering them food. *Jesa* takes place on the evening before the anniversary of the one who passed away. A family could have multiple *jesa* in a year. This family affair brings together the relatives and a stronger sense of family kinship develops through sharing the offered food for the dead. Additionally, *charae* has the same proceedings as *jesa*, but it is to thank the ancestors for family's continuous well-being and prosperity. *Charae* is carried out on the morning of Lunar New Year's day and *Chuseok*.

4 Koreans' Love for Children

Koreans' love for their children is so strong, often to the point of excessive. Koreans typically have very strong love for their families and this is even more so when it comes to their children. However, the Korean way of doting on children is very different from that of Westerners. When Koreans see children, they think they are so cute that they will often touch or pat them. These acts stem from a desire to show interest and love for a child's innocence and beauty. If someone in a subway tries to touch a Westerner's child, the parent will immediately think, "That person is weird," but Korean have deep trust in relationships between adults and children and therefore do not associate such behavior negatively.

Because of Koreans' indiscriminate love for children, there are times when it becomes problematic in public places. Children may run around recklessly and shout loudly in public places such as restaurants or churches. Some parents will do nothing to control this behavior of their children. If someone tries to stop the children, the parents may even say, "They are just children. Leave them alone." Such situations are acknowledged to be a social problem and even Koreans are trying to fix this behavior, although it is not something that can be fixed overnight.

5 Practical Application Tip

In a Korean company or organizations, the phrase "We are family" is often used. What does this mean? It means they want their organization to become one, just like a family, and dedicate oneself to the organization as though it were one's own family.

But today's younger generation has a different mindset; personal preferences are strong, and many times, young people will not comply with the demands of the organization. Korean companies are aware of this trend and are trying to change their organizational culture accordingly.

Confirming What You've Learned

One day, your Korean friend says he will introduce you to "our" mother. So you go over to your friend's house and your Korean friend introduces you to his mother. He refers you as his best friend in "our" company. Why does your Korean friend keep using the word "our"?

Expert Opinion Koreans view the group they are associated with as the smallest social unit. Therefore, since one is not alone, one can refer to things as "ours." On the other hand, Westerners view the smallest unit as the "individual," so things can be referred to as "mine." Even when referring to things pertaining to "me," the word "our" is used, as in our house, our mom, our school, and our company. This illustrates the point that Koreans think of themselves as being small groups, rather than being alone.

3

Friends

In Korea, this term is only used between those of a similar age, in the same school or university class, or coworkers who joined the company at the same time. "Similar age" means people within a year or two of one's own age. Thus, the word "friend" has a much more limited meaning in Korea than it has in the West. Of course, one may form friendship with those more than two years senior or junior to them, however they would not be called "friends."

As discussed in Chapter 1, friendships in Korea usually result from school or work relationships. In the Western world, the term "friend" could mean many different things than to Koreans such as an elementary school teacher, a close neighbor, an upperclassman, or a more experienced workmate.

Who would you usually refer to as a "friend"? Who would Koreans refer to as a "friend"? Pick from the choices below.

1) Your neighborhood grocer whom you know very well
2) Your hairdresser at a salon you visit frequently
3) The female owner of a restaurant you visit two to three times a week
4) An old friend of your own age whom you have known since you were little.

In Western culture, all of the above may be a friend, but in Korean culture, only 4) is the answer for a friend.

1 System of Social Organization

Before we further examine the Korean concept of "friend," let us first look at how social organizations are formed. There are two types of social organization systems worldwide. One is based on kinship and the other is based on association.

The kinship method is often visible in Latin America and in Asian countries such as Korea, China, and Japan. One becomes relatives through marriages and a relative of a relative becomes one's own relatives. Members of the same group share feelings and a sense of belonging to the extended family and give a sense of responsibility to the family. In Korea, this sense of kinship is unique becuase it is not reserved only for relatives but can include alumni of the same school or colleagues in the same organization.

An associative system of social organization can often be seen in Europe or the United States. Organizations are formed based on age, gender, or a common interest. However, because such organizations are formed based on mutual understanding of others, strong bonds typically do not form.

In comparison, social organizations based on kinship have much stronger bonds. Of course, even in Korea there are organizations that are associative. A company is a prime example of an associative type of organization. However, even within this type of organization there can be smaller groups that form based on kinship. These small groups can become strong informal organizations that have great influence on communication as well.

2 Concept of a Friend

As seen earlier, to be friends in a Korean community, you must be of similar age, background and interest to maintain lateral relationship. Hence, friends are often classmates or childhood friends from the same neighborhood. At work, coworkers of similar age and positions can become friends.

For example, at school you would never call an upperclassman a friend, but would rather use the title "senior" (*seonbae*). If you call an upperclassman or a former advisor a friend, you will be considered as someone without manners.

In the West, anyone who is more than an acquaintance can be called a friend, but that is not the case in Korea. To call anyone a friend in Korea shows a lack of courtesy. However, any Korean who has had experiences abroad knows of this difference, so using the term "friend" amongst such friends is not a problem.

For the most part, the ages of the students in the same class are all the same, but conflicts can arise when students have different age in a given grade. In such cases, the two involved in the conflict should resolve the problem, or a mutual friend can offer a solution. If such matters are not resolved properly, the two parties in the conflict can turn into enemies and violence may arise.

Case Study

Conflict Situation in the School

A fight broke out between two Korean high school students, 17 and 19 year-olds, at a high school in Los Angeles in the United States. Both of these students were transfer students studying abroad from Korea. The incident started because the 19-year-old student demanded that the 17-year-old student to call him "*Hyung*" (older brother) since he was older, but the 17-year-old refused. The fight between the two students happened suddenly and resulted in the 19-year-old injuring his head badly. Although he was taken to a hospital emergency room, he eventually died. Currently, the other student is being held in a juvenile center and is expected to be tried for murder.

As seen earlier, friendship is only possible in an equal, lateral relationship in Korea. However, even if age or position is similar, if one side becomes disproportionately successful or fails miserably and ruins the equivalent nature of the relationship, the friendship can easily be ruined as well. Because Koreans have such a strong notion of being equals, if the basis for equality in a relationship is ruined, it can cause a breakdown in their friendship as well.

4
Education

Koreans are very passionate about education. They have their own unique educational method, which has significant influence in forming their mentality. Let us now examine why Koreans view education as so important and how that affects the lives of Koreans.

1 Koreans' Strong Passion for Education

To understand the current Korean education system, we need to understand how Koreans have viewed education in the past. Koreans venerate studying and have a very strong passion for education. This was because education was the only way to improve one's social status. In the past, to become a government official, one needed to pass a state examination. Thus, the exam was a crucial, life-changing event.

Let us consider the Korean caste system. Although the caste system existed in Korea about 1000 years ago, it only became systemized and stipulated during the *Joseon* Era in 1392. During the *Joseon* Era, there was a caste nobility system. The nobility system was divided into four different classes consisting nobles (*yangban*), a middle class, civilians, and lower class. The noble class was not a status you could achieve through hard work, but was only inherited. There was a strict differentiation of the classes and movement between the classes was virtually impossible. Nobles were the ruling class in *Joseon*. They studied Confucianism and took exams to become government officials who led the country. The middle class was lower than the nobles and consisted of those that showed talent in medicine and technology. They often worked in government agencies that were designated to assist the nobles. Civilians were the majority of the people and usually participated in farming, trading, and manufacturing. Finally, the lower class usually worked as servants to the nobles or worked on tasks that deemed too arduous or dangerous for others.

Participation in the state exams (*gwageo*) to become bureaucrats was not open to all classes. Only nobles (*yangban*) were allowed to partake in such exams, while the middle class and civilians could only take tests for certain subjects and skills. It was extremely rare for anyone in the lower class to take any exams.

As the *Joseon* Era came to an end and the Japanese Colonial Period began, the noble class system fell apart, leaving all Koreans suddenly in equal status to each other. Suddenly, an opportunity to increase one's status had opened. However, even then only those with higher education were given the opportunity to work in government offices. For these reasons, the idea that education is the only way to increase status was further reinforced in Korea. The passionate pursuit of education followed, with families selling their livestock and farmland in order to educate their children. Because most people were farmers at the time, selling your land and livestock meant selling your whole fortune. Therefore, colleges became known as cow-bone towers rather than ivory towers.

Korea is a country where the correlation of education and income is very high. So the parents' decision to invest in their children by selling livestock to educate was common. Because obtaining a job in Korea is determined by educational level, those with less education find it difficult to move to a higher position, thus restricting their income level. Therefore, Korean parents want to provide the best education for their children. Elementary school is mandatory, and only few (less than 5 percent) do not finish secondary education (middle and high school). In addition, because 79 percent of high school graduates go to college, the college acceptance rate is very high and many even attend graduate school afterwards.[1]

2 Koreans' Admiration of Academia

To see whom a nation respects, we only need to look at the nation's bills (or banknotes). In Western countries such as United States or the United Kingdom, presidents, kings or queens are portrayed, but in Korea respected scholars are portrayed on the bills.

Korean has four denominations of bills: 1,000 won, 5,000 won, 10,000 won, and 50,000 won. On the 1,000 won bill, Yi Hwang, a 16th century Confucian scholar who founded a prominent academy for fellow scholars, is featured. On the 5,000 won bill, a Confucian thinker and politician Yi I is portrayed. Yi I was also known as the Saint (Scholar) of the East. On the 10,000 won bill, King Sejong, the creator of *Hangul*, the Korean alphabet and the greatest scholar of all time, is presented. On the 50,000 won bill, a famous female scholar and artist of the *Joseon* Era, Sin Saimdang, is printed. All four Korean bills feature scholars and this shows how much Koreans value and respect the academia and its scholars. You may wonder how King Sejong is considered a scholar. Not only did he invented *Hangul*, but he also encouraged scientists to invent sundial, rain gauge and other scientific discoveries during his time.

3 Koreans' Way of Education

The Korean educational system is very different from the West. When we compared the differences between the East and West in Chapter 2, we learned that Westerners emphasize logical thinking. Westerners think that knowledge is gained through conversations and discussions and that learning takes place in environments where teachers and students to freely communicate with each other.

However, most Asian countries with Confucian-based education system, including Korea, view that knowledge is passed on by a teacher. Thus, learning takes place more through one-sided lectures than through conversations or discussions. Furthermore, the social emphasis on hierarchy and seniority makes it even more challenging to learn through discussions. Under Confucianism, the king, teachers, and parents are at the same level and should be regarded with utmost respect and questioning them is considered disrespectful. While it is acceptable and allowed for students to ask questions when they do not know or understand, it is unacceptable and almost forbidden to show different opinion or debate with the teacher. Presenting a different opinion than his or her superior in the company is viewed equivalently as trying to debate with a teacher at school. This is why it is difficult to have discussions at work with people of various positions and ranks in Asia.

In the Western world, students are educated under the principle "There is no absolute truth," which allows them to challenge existing truth to gain more knowledge. Eastern education teaches that it's better to listen and follow the advice of an old sage. For example, stating that Confucius' teachings are skewed would cause a major social uproar.

On the other hand, this type of education system has its benefits as well. Since students study in a repetitive manner under established structure, subjects are learned much more effectively. However, students often lack creativity. While Koreans have outstanding aptitude until high school, there is much room for improvement in creativity.

How we can relate these educational differences to business situation? In the hierarchy-centered Korean culture that revolves around the position and seniority, trying to have a discussion among people of varying positions is often difficult. This is because Koreans do not want to state an opinion that might contradict the opinion of their superior. Therefore, Koreans tend to find comfort in following the directions of a superior than to try to find solutions through discussions. Also, instead of taking the initiative to try to find new solutions to solve problems, Koreans tend to rely on a precedent. If they cannot find precedent within their own organization, they will look to other companies for benchmarking. When a subordinate suggests a new solution, the Korean superior's first question will likely be, "What did we do in the past?" or "Have we done that before?"

Confirming What You've Learned

A new Korean superior has been appointed in your office. There is not much information about the new superior. You are a very active marketing manager in your company. While discussing a newly launched product with your peers, you thought of a very innovative marketing strategy. Your peers agreed that the idea was very good and that it was worth giving it a try. However, you have to explain your idea to the newly appointed Korean superior with whom you are not very familiar with. How would you explain your plan to your superior and persuade him to launch it?

Expert Opinion Besides the fact that he is Korean, there is not much else you know about your new superior. Instead of presenting your opinion too aggressively, carefully explain your new idea, the motivation behind the idea and why it is worth to launch it. Also explaining what risks are involved is a good idea.

When most Koreans try to adjust to a new organization, they are often very careful. Therefore, your new superior may not want to immediately take a risk by undertaking a new and challenging project. He may ask you if you have done similar work in the past. Or he may ask if the method you are suggesting has been adopted by another company. To convince him, you need to take into consideration his personality and his background. Of course, the newly appointed superior may love challenges; however, there is no harm in carefully preparing your plans.

---

5 Language

1 Korean Language

Korean is currently the national language for both South and North Korea and is used by approximately 78 million people in these countries, as well as 7 million Koreans abroad. Also, the Korean language is ranked 13th in the number of speakers among the 6,000 existing languages worldwide.[2]

2 History of *Hangul*

The Korean writing system is called *Hangul*. When, by whom, and how was *Hangul* created? Up until the *Joseon* Dynasty, Koreans had no writing system of their own and had to use Chinese characters which were very complex, and difficult to learn. Koreans had their own spoken language but they had to borrow the complex Chinese characters to express their spoken language. Only nobles were able to learn and acquire knowledge and for commoners it was very difficult to become literate.

In 1443, during King Sejong's rule, *Hangul* was invented so the common people could learn to write with ease. As a result, the common people were able to become literate and enriching their lives. When King Sejong invented *Hangul*, he faced strong opposition from the nobles and officials because they felt they might lose their power if commoners were able to read and share written information. However, King Sejong overcame the opposition and completed the development of *Hangul*.

In all of human history, no other king of a nation or any individual invented a written language for his people. Because *Hangul* was created with such a clear purpose, it is also very practical. *Hangul* was invented to help the poor and uneducated citizens to easily learn and use it to communicate in writing as well. The alphabet system evolved from a 28-letter to a 24-letter today and it is the greatest Korean heritage.

Now, how do foreigners rate *Hangul*?

A: Unlike English or French, Korean is a unique language you can learn easily. Learning how to read Korean takes only a day, so *Hangul* is a writing system that is both very scientific and convenient to communicate with.

B: King Sejong invented a unique and amazing writing system

called *Hangul* for his people. *Hangul* is the most scientific writing system that you cannot find anywhere else in the world.

C: *Hangul* is the ultimate alphabet that all languages dream to be.

D: King Sejong achieved the Western phonetics theory of the 20th century five centuries earlier. *Hangul* is the ultimate writing system that combines traditional philosophy and scientific theories.

When *Hangul* was created, it was called "*Hunminjeongeum*," which means "the correct sound to teach the peoples." It was a language for the people and anyone could easily learn with its simple alphabets.

3 Convenience of *Hangul*

All writing systems around the world can be divided into ideographs and phonetic letters. With ideographs, each letter has a specific meaning, Chinese characters being the prime example. However, trying to memorize all of those letters is not an easy task. On the other hand, phonetic letters do not require as many letters. Like the English alphabet, *Hangul* is a phonetic alphabet, making it easier to learn. Since each letter represents a specific sound, you can easily make a wide variety of sounds by putting the letters together.

4 Scientific Principles in the Creation of *Hangul*

The basic design principle behind *Hangul* is very simple. The Korean alphabet can be written using only the basic outline of a triangle, a circle, a square, a dot, and a straight line. The basic consonants shapes were modeled after speech organ shapes and the shapes of the vowel were based on the sky, the land, and human. Adding brush strokes is also a principle that further differentiates *Hangul*. The basic letter ㄱ(giyeok) can be made into ㄲ(ssang giyeok) by adding another ㄱ(giyeok) or simply adding a line to ㄱ (giyeok) makes ㅋ(kieuk), resulting in the new letters that produce harsher and stronger sound.

Hangul is made of 14 consonants and 10 vowels. When certain lines are added, the number of consonants and vowels increases, but we will only learn about the basic alphabets in this chapter. Each consonant and each vowel has its own unique sound property. The word "butterfly" in English is written as 나비(nah-bi) in *Hangul*. The consonant ㄴ(n) is written with the vowel ㅏ(a) to form 나(nah), and the consonant ㅂ(b) is written with the vowel ㅣ(i) to form 비 (bi).

The reason *Hangul* is easy to read is because each letter of the alphabet has only one sound. In English, the letter "a" can sometimes be pronounced as "a" or other times as "ah," but in *Hangul* the vowel that is the equivalent of the letter "a," ㅏ(a) is always pronounced as "a." This means that if one can read Korean, upon receiving someone's business card, one can pronounce the person's name correctly. This is not always the case in other languages.

5 Honorifics

In Korean, your relationship with the person you are talking to, the situation and the location will determine whether to use honorifics or not. The Korean language has one of the most complex honorific systems in the world. Both grammar and vocabulary change when honorifics are used, requiring careful attention in any given situation. Although using wrong honorific can be considered extremely rude, Koreans are very forgiving of misusing honorific rules for foreigners because Koreans know that this is the most difficult part of learning the language for foreigners.

Honorific are used to talk up to or down to the person with whom you are speaking. Hence, honorifics express differences in status or differences in intimacy. Social rank, age, social position, kinship, gender differences, and intimacy level will determine the appropriate honorific.

6 Practicality of *Hangul*

Hangul was created very scientifically, making it very easy to learn. Some scholars view *Hangul* as the most advanced alphabet of a spoken language. *Hangul* contributed greatly to Korea's ranking at the 9th place in worldwide information communication rankings. It also helped Korea to secure its place as a leader in the worldwide IT industry. The systematic form of *Hangul* enables work efficiently with the 12 keys on a cellular phone or the 60 keys on a computer keyboard. Moreover, inputting *Hangul* on a cellular phone was found to be 35 percent faster than English and productivity levels when using *Hangul* on a computer are found to be 7 times higher than using Chinese or Japanese characters.[3]

7 *Hangul* as a Worldwide Inheritance beyond Korea

Although *Hangul* was created more than 570 years ago, the practical advancement of the system has happened in the last 100 years. Despite its short history, *Hangul* now stands proudly in the world. Some American and Australian colleges designated Korean as their second language, and many Korean companies with international branches in Asia and Eastern Europe are having their employees learn Korean as well.

About 6,000 languages exist in the world today and many of these are spoken by small ethnic groups with no written alphabet. Korea is fighting illiteracy in these small ethnic groups by spreading *Hangul*, so they can use it to write their own language and decrease illiteracy. In Bau-Bau, a small city on Buton Island off the southeast coast of Sulawesi, live the Jjia-Jjia (or Cia-Cia) people who speak their native tongue of Jjia-Jjia. However, for hundreds of years they could not leave any written records because they did not have a written alphabet. To remedy this, *Hangul* was selected as the written alphabet for the Jjia-Jjia language and have been used in their education since 2009.

Moving beyond a writing system, *Hangul* has been recognized recently for its beauty in art and culture as well. *Hangul* is truly becoming a world heritage, touching the lives of people around the world. In 1997, UNESCO registered *Hunminjeongeum* — the original *Hangul* — as the "Memory of the World" and created UNESCO King Sejong Literacy Prize to recognize those fighting illiteracy each year.

6
Clothing, Food, and Housing

1 Environmentally-Friendly Clothing, Food, and Housing

The most important aspect in clothing, food, and housing of Korea is that they are environmentally friendly. Since long ago, Koreans believed in the importance of living in nature without harming nature. Such environmental friendliness played an important role in what Korean people ate and wore.

2 Clothing

Koreans believe that one can determine a person's personality, position in society or personal preferences by looking at how they dress. Since long ago, clothing differentiated classes and gender, and was an instrument to show formality or courtesy. As one's status increased, more extravagant and colorful materials like silk were used in clothing and accessories. Unmarried singles wore their hair in long braids while married men and women wore their hair in a bun. One's status and class were shown through one's appearance. An old Korean adage says, "Clothing is your wings." This figuratively shows the importance of clothing. That is, how you dress can change your appearance and impression. These days, traditional Korean *hanbok* is only worn during New Years and other holidays, or major family occasions. This is partly because *hanbok* is not very fit for the active lifestyle of today, but modernized *hanbok* has gained popularity recently.

Korea's four distinct seasons requires a lot of clothing compared to countries with little climate change. Since Koreans are very sensitive to fashion trends, they often consume more clothing than other countries. Also, as we learned in Chapter 1, Koreans view dressing appropriately is important and is part of saving "face." These reasons helped foster development in the clothing industries in Korea.

3 Food

Korean food revolves around rice which is accompanied by soup and side dishes. All dishes are brought at once to a large table. This is different from Western foods, which are generally served in courses. In the Korean table setting, rice is placed to the left of the diner, while the soup is placed to the right, and the spoon and chopsticks are placed to the right of the soup bowl. Since all food is shared at the table, one must to be mindful not to unnecessarily stir the food with chopsticks and not to only eat the side dishes or *banchan* that one may like. Koreans believe eating a wide variety of food is good for health and these table manners are taught to children when they are young.

Koreans believe that the proper balance of nutrition is important. That is why many *banchan* is prepared to eat along with the rice so people can consume wide variety of food. Traditionally, wealthy Koreans had more than 30 *banchan* on their table, and over 100 different ingredients were used to prepare those foods.

Korea has four seasons with widely varying temperatures which made storing food very difficult. So in order to preserve food, fermented food became common in Korean cuisine. The most famous fermented food is *kimchi*, a side dish that cannot be absent from a Korean's table. Containing healthy probiotics and nutrients, this fermented side dish is included in the top ten longevity foods of the world and is known worldwide. There are over 200 different types of *kimchi*, including the common spicy and red *kimchi*, white *kimchi*, cucumber *kimchi*, and wrap *kimchi*. Many foreigners enjoy *kimchi* these days.

Besides *kimchi*, other popular Korean foods include *bibimbap*, *bulgogi*, and *japchae*. All three are foods that foreigners enjoy very much. How many ingredients go into one dish? *Bibimbap* has meat, zucchini, onions, eggs, carrots, and other root vegetables in a bowl. These ingredients are mixed with a rich redpepper sauce over rice. *Bulgogi* is marinated beef with various seasonings and carrots, onions, green onions, and a variety of mushrooms. *Japchae* is made of noodles with carrots, meat, onions, spinach, mushrooms, and many other ingredients. These foods are excellent sources of nutrition and boast a variety of flavors, textures, and colors that complement each other to bring joy to both mouth and eyes.

Korean eat differently from other countries. Even in China, a close neighbor, a big main dish is served and each diner serves themselves in their individual plate. Like China, most Western countries also serve their food in a main dish. In Japan, all food is served individually. On the other hand, Koreans serve their soup and rice individually, while everything else is shared with others. This means that everyone's utensils go into the same dish. Being able to share a meal like this indicates the closeness between those sharing a meal.

To Westerners this may seem unhygienic, but Koreans do not view it as so. In Koreans' social relationships, sharing a meal indicates a level of closeness. However, such dining culture may be uncomfortable for foreigners. When sharing a meal, saying "I do not want to put my spoon in the same bowl" outright may cause hurt feelings or distance in relationships. Therefore, if sharing food is something one is not comfortable with, asking for a personal plate may be a better way to indirectly express your discomfort. In fact, Koreans are becoming increasingly aware of hygiene issues from sharing foods that the trend nowadays is to serve food on personal plates.

Confirming What You've Learned

When Koreans meet, they often ask each other if they've eaten. This form of greeting is not used when you first meet someone, but rather after you've met them at least twice or have become close. Why is asking someone if they ate become a form of a common greeting?

Expert Opinion This is because, from the *Joseon* Dynasty, through the Japanese occupation and until the late 1960s, many Koreans struggled to survive. Therefore, to Koreans, eating has grown to have very special meaning. They like to hold meetings with foods or have meetings over meals with acquaintances. Sharing food plays a very important role in forming and maintaining a bond to Koreans.

---

4 Housing

A traditional Korean house is a wooden structure with wood and mud used in the framework, walls and floors. Tiles and hay are used for the roof because the earthen walls absorb moisture while blocking out the cold air. This was a very practical housing solution for Korea's four distinct seasons. The heating was provided through *ondol*, heated stone floor. *Ondol* heats the floor with hot air produced from the furnace and allows for optimal heat transfer and ventilation.

Modern housing became more common in Korea but some characteristics of the traditional Korean housing remain. Most houses still heat their rooms through the floor, use environmentally friendly clay for the walls, and even use traditional paper as wallpapers. One can also easily find modern buildings that combine the traditional and modern building techniques.

Because land is scarce in Korea, many Koreans live in apartment buildings today. Traditionally, Koreans lived in separate houses, but due to a high population density and overcrowding, high-rise apartment buildings were introduced in the 1970s. In the past, large families lived together in big houses but with the advent of the modern nuclear family, it became more common to live in smaller apartments that are suitable for smaller families in today's society. Also, the design of the traditional *hanok* posed security problems, so apartments gained popularity. As a result, apartments are currently the most popular form of housing in Korea, with approximately 50 percent of Koreans living in them.

Now let us look at the floor heating system of Korea. We learned about Korea's climate and that the Korean winters are very cold. Therefore, a heating system is essential. The "*Ondol*" heating system warms the floors and was designed to enable sitting on the floor. Unlike Westerners, Koreans take off their shoes indoors and walk around bare feet or with socks at home. Although many now use beds, traditionally, thick blankets were laid out on the floor, which required warm floors during the colder months. Westerners generally cover the cold floor with carpet but Korean *hanok* typically has wooden floors that easily transfer heat. Houses made with clay emit beneficial infrared rays when heated through the *ondol* system.

Some still build their houses this way, but most people use a *jjimjilbang*. *Jjimjilbang* is a Korean sauna equipped with various types of sauna rooms, each with a different temperature, and a public bath. Among these saunas at a *jjimjilbang* is the clay sauna. Additionally, there are salt saunas, jade saunas, amethyst saunas, and even charcoal saunas. If you go to a Korean sauna, you can see all of the saunas that are said to be good for your body! Additionally, there are different recreation areas within the *jjimjilbang* that are cater to men and women, old and young. You can also enjoy delicious food as well. If there is ever a chance to visit a Korea, visiting sauna is recommended. A trip to the *jjimjilbang* will be an experience in many different aspects of Korean culture in a short period of time.

Summary of Chapter 3

1. Age

- Age is a very important factor when interacting with Koreans in social or business environment.
- For Koreans, age is something that humans cannot control and therefore is the fairest standard within the human community.
- Because of this, the Korean organizational hierarchy is typically determined based on seniority unless special circumstances exist.

2. Family

- Western conception of family emphasizes the importance of family-centered life and quality family time.
- Koreans also love their family, but they believe that each family member has a unique role within the family and fulfilling that role to the best of their abilities is ultimately what is best for the family.

3. Friends

- To be friends with a Korean, you must be of similar age, background, and interest in order to keep a lateral relationship.
- The term "friend" in Korea is only used between those of a similar age, same class, or coworkers of a similar rank. Compared to the West, the term "friend" is restricted to a much smaller demographic. While friendships are possible between two individuals with a large age gap, they would not be called "friends" in Korea.

4. Education

- Koreans are very passionate about education and have a unique educational system.
- From their passion for education, Korea has a highly qualified workforce which became the driving force for Korea's astonishing economic development in such a short period of time.

5. Language

- *Hangul*, the Korean alphabet system, was invented by King Sejong approximately 570 years ago to help people learn and write with ease.

6. Clothing, Food, and Housing

- Koreans believe that one can determine a person's personality and level of culture, position in society or personal preferences by the way they dress.
- Korean food revolves around rice that is accompanied by soup and side dishes. All dishes are brought at once to a large table.
- A traditional Korean house is a wooden structure with wood and mud used in the framework, walls and floors. Tiles and hay are used for the roof. Because earthen walls absorb moisture while blocking out the cold air, it is the very practical housing solution for Korea's four distinct seasons.
- Heating was provided through heated stone under the floors which allowed good ventilation.

Chapter 04

Business in Korea

In this chapter, we will cover cases involving real business life in Korea. Cultural differences are inevitably manifested in business processes and learning to understand these differences is a fundamental key for success in global business. In this chapter, we will cover the basic etiquette and manners when first meeting a Korean businessperson. We will also briefly compare these differences with other countries.

First, let us take a look at etiquette and manners. The concepts of manners and etiquette are often confused because they are not clearly distinguished. What is the exact difference between manners and etiquette? Etiquette is defined as rules to be abided by in social life. Manners are defined as the characteristic or customary way of acting in social settings. The term etiquette is used to denote rational standard of human social behavior and manners are the physical expression of these standards of behavior.

Etiquettes are not legally binding but are regulatory guidelines that should be abided by to facilitate smooth and pleasant social life. In other words, etiquette is a kind of a social promise, a way of extending kindness towards others. Etiquette is not something acquired overnight. Being aware and considerate of others and their surroundings as well as trying to behave according to these thoughts slowly lend their ways to one's acquiring of etiquette. Etiquettes generally vary by regions and countries as well as their cultures and customs. Therefore, learning each other's culture, lifestyle and social systems is necessary for understanding etiquette.

Let us look at some examples of the different etiquettes in the East and West. In the East, people usually knock when entering an open stall in a public toilet while people in the West normally do not. This is because there is usually a space at the bottom of Western bathroom stall which enables people to see if it is occupied. Knocking may even be considered a disturbance in such cases. As you can see, difference in Eastern and Western etiquettes are manifested differently. However, in terms of manners, these different behaviors are all born out of respect and consideration for others. That is, while etiquette and manners differ slightly in their definitions, they both ultimately provide a judge of one's character and level of sophistication.

In today's society, having good manners are not only necessary in building social relationships but also in business exchanges. Furthermore, as our societies grow more complex and exchanges between individuals, corporations and nations become more common place, being mindful of appropriate manners and etiquette in business is growing in its importance.

1

Making an Appointment

Now, let us take a look at the manners and etiquette of Koreans in business settings. It goes without saying that Koreans should be well prepared for the business cultures and etiquettes of their foreign business partners as well. However, this chapter will focus on Korean manners and etiquettes.

Nothing is more important than first impressions. Whether at work or in other situations, first impression is important because it can greatly influence future interactions. This is why first meetings are important for everyone. Koreans believe first meetings are extremely important, especially for business, because it can determine how the relationship will form. As mentioned in previous chapters, Koreans emphasize relationship in many aspects, which is why first meetings can greatly influence how smooth future business exchange will be.

Now, let us look at how to arrange meetings with Koreans. Typically, Koreans will schedule appointments about two weeks in advance when meeting for the first time. When trying to meet with an executive, scheduling through an assistant is standard. In absence of an assistant, it is acceptable to directly contact by phone or by e-mail. When scheduling a meeting with an acquaintance, one could even schedule a last minute meeting, i.e. the following day. However, in the Czech Republic, two weeks buffer is standard even for well-acquainted partners.

If one is visiting temporarily Korea on business, it is more than likely that meetings may be scheduled within one week of initiating contact. Koreans are generally very accommodating to those who will travel far to visit. Traditionally Koreans show considerable hospitality for guests from afar, which is why they may expect the same level of accommodation when visiting other countries, by trying to schedule meetings with short notice.

Korean businessmen typically expect that a junior person will be flexible to the superiors' schedule. Again, this is because of the hierarchical nature of Koreans. A meeting with a superior should be scheduled through formal channels, however one may arrange through informal channels if they are well acquainted. Furthermore, if the meeting is mutually considered very important, appointments can be scheduled on weekends and holidays as well.

If there is a mutual acquaintance, it is recommended that meetings are arranged with the acquaintance's introduction. Because relationships are so important and Koreans value common connection, having a mutual acquaintance could instantly provide a connection to facilitate smoother relationship building and help establish credibility with the new business partner.

Imagine that you are an engineer in the UK. You have to meet Mr. Kim, the marketing director in Dubai, whom you have never met before. Of course, you can contact Mr. Kim directly and set up an appointment for the meeting. However, if you have never met Mr. Kim before, it might be in your best interest to schedule a meeting through a coworker in the UK who might know Mr. Kim very well. Again, this is because Koreans value relationships. When choosing a mutual acquaintance for a referral or introduction, it is important to consider who is introducing you. Because the mutual acquaintance's credibility becomes synonymous to your own credibility, it is important to consider how important your contact is to your future business partner.

Koreans generally try to be punctual for meetings. A five-minute grace period is usually acceptable, but being late is not looked upon favorably. However, because Korea's metropolitan areas have heavy traffic, out-of-town guests are usually given more leeway in appointment times. When visiting metropolitan areas in Korea, it would be wise to factor in plenty of travel time to account for heavy traffic. If being late to a meeting is unavoidable, it is good practice to call ahead and apologize at least ten minutes in advance. Because mobile phone use is ubiquitous in Korea, Koreans expect such courtesy call in the face of unexpected delay.

Case Study

Be Puncture

As a representative of your Company, you have arranged a meeting with a Mexican client company. In order to ensure a successful start to the project, you have decided to gather some information. After the meeting, you will examine additional information gathered at today's meeting and report to headquarters. Today, you have scheduled a 10:00 am meeting with 10 Mexican managers at their company.

You arrive at the conference room at 9:50 am and it is now 10:15 am. Although the meeting was scheduled for 10:00 am, only two people have showed up. At 10:20 am, a third manager arrives to inform you that the rest of the managers will not be attending the meeting. At 10:25 am another manager arrives. What would you do in this situation?

Expert Opinion Begin by making light conversation with the three managers while you wait for at least fifteen more minutes. If the remaining managers do not arrive, you should offer to reschedule the meeting. We can see here that there are cultural differences in punctuality.

Mexicans do not have the same understanding on punctuality as Koreans or maybe even people in your home country. Also punctuality and work capability may not be considered relevant. Therefore, not attending your meeting does not necessarily mean that these managers do not think the project is important. In such a case, the most effective route would be to reiterate the importance of the meeting to gain their support and reschedule the meeting.

2

Meetings

Koreans introduce the members of their group by name and position in order of hierarchy. Introductions should not be done according to the order in which people are standing. Instead, instruction by the order of hierarchy (depending on the situation, it could be the rank order of job position, seniority or order by date of graduation from university) is advisable when dealing with Koreans.

Typically, when meeting at a partner's or a client's company, visitors typically wait in the meeting rooms. When meeting for the first time, both parties will bow and introduce themselves and exchange business cards. Handshakes often follow, although not always for women.

When Koreans do not know the order of hierarchy in a foreign group, they will automatically begin with the eldest looking person. Therefore, a person who looks older but may in fact be junior sometimes can be greeted first, based on physical appearance. If there is any possibility of such confusion, it is advisable that the visiting party introduce itself first, starting with the most senior person. If Koreans later find out that they made mistake in the order of introduction, they will be embarrassed of this mistake.

Greetings are the first step in getting to know one another and express hospitality and respect. Proper greetings can signal a sense of confidence and foster amicable relationships. In Korea, greetings are exchanged with bows. There are three basic types of bows.

The least formal is used in casual settings, which involves a slight lowering of the eyes, with bowing forward about 15 degrees. This greeting is used most often among coworkers, toward junior employees, and amongst frequent acquaintances. This bow can also be used when casually thanking someone. A deeper, 30-degree bow is a standard bow that is used most often with clients or with seniors. A full 45-degree bow is the most polite bow and is used to express deep thanks, apologies, or for situations involving familial elders or executives.

When Koreans exchange business cards, they usually present them using both hands, with the visiting party usually offering its cards first. However, many Koreans with foreign experience generally understand when foreigners present their cards with single hand and they will do likewise. When handing business cards to superiors, it is polite to hand the card with both hands (the use of two hands is a sign of respect), with the left hand under the right. This also applies when pouring drinks; one hand supports the other when pouring.

It is important to handle the received business cards with care. Handling business cards with care is a sign of respect. Fidgeting with a business card during a meeting or forgetting to keep someone's business card could seriously damage one's first impression. During meetings, one can place cards in a wallet or on the table to help remember names. In Korea, business cards usually show the person's name, title, and company name. Having a business card printed in both Korean and English (one side in English and the other in Korean) will be well received by Korean companies and will make a good first impression.

The seating arrangement is also an important form of etiquette in Korea. In general, Koreans are very sensitive to the seating arrangement at meetings. When two parties meet, each party will typically sit across from each other on either side of the table. Having name cards or seating charts are good ways to avoid confusion. If the seating arrangement is unclear, it is a good idea to ask your Korean counterpart. This applies to table etiquette as well.

Case Study

Seating Arrangements

You are an assistant manager in the marketing team. Your team is launching a new product and you are in charge of hosting a dinner for the marketing team and your advertising company. The marketing director, manager and you will attend the dinner while the director, manager and an assistant from the advertising company will attend. With a total of six people attending, how should you arrange the seating for the dinner?

Expert Opinion Seating arrangements are an important aspect of entertaining guests and you need to know which the prime seating is. In personal gatherings, seating can be more flexible but in business settings, it is important to keep the proper seating order in mind and offer prime seating according to hierarchy.

First, based on status hierarchy, the highest ranking person will take the prime seat. Second, based on seniority, the oldest person will take the prime seat. If the oldest person has lower rank, hierarchy of rank takes precedence. Third, women are given prime seating over men, all other things being equal.

So where is the prime seat? It depends on the location and its surroundings, but there are several rules on distinguishing the prime seat. First, a seat that has the wall behind its back is considered a prime seat, rather than those that face the wall. Second, a seat that is farther away from the entrance is considered a prime seat while those closer to the entrance are considered the lowest seats. Third, seats with better views are prime seats. Fourth, seats closer to the prime seats as defined above are considered better seats and seats farther away from the prime seat are considered lower seats.

Let us take a look at how Koreans shake hands. Handshakes are an important part of social life because they express mutual affection. In general, the more senior person will initiate a handshake. Also, a handshake will be offered from higher rank to lower rank, woman to a man, senior to a junior and customer to an employee.

As a rule of thumb, handshakes are done using the right hand only. The grip should be suitably firm and shaken moderately high. Some Koreans will bow their heads or cup the other's hand with their left hand. This is an Eastern tradition that signals respect, so it should not be taken as an offense. Some women may choose not to shake hands and bow instead. This practice originates from the Confucian culture in Korea and should not be taken as a sign of disrespect.

Now, let us take a look at how to address others in a business setting. When Koreans are introduced, it is usually considered rude to call the person by their given name. In general, Koreans place their family name first, which is followed by their two-syllabled, given name. Using the title Mr., Mrs., or Miss and the last name is generally an acceptable way of addressing someone.

For example, a man named Kim Minsoo has family name of Kim and given name of Minsoo. He would be addressed as Mr. Kim. If Kim Minsoo is a doctor or professor, he may be called Dr. Kim or

Professor Kim. Because doctors and professors are highly respected occupations in Korea, some may find it flattering to be addressed by their occupations.

People are usually addressed by their family name followed by a formal title. Adding the honorific *nim* is also very important. Therefore, a person with the family name Kim and the title *sajang* (meaning CEO in Korean) would be addressed as "Kim *sajang nim*." Addressing Korean business partners with this Korean custom will generate a very positive response.

When unsure of how to address a Korean partner, it is appropriate to ask the person how he/she would like to be addressed. Calling a person by their first name is generally considered rude in formal settings and is often reserved for close friends only. In fact, even close friends will call each other by their formal titles in public, formal settings. However those familiar with Western cultures will be more tolerant of being called by their given names and understand that it is a sign of closeness and friendship.

Many Koreans share same family names. One out of every five Koreans has the family name Kim. There are approximately 250 different family names in Korea. The names have various origins as started in the Three Kingdoms Period, family genealogies, or *jokbo*, were systemized during the *Goryeo* Dynasty.

Most Korean family names have only one syllable and few have two. The five most common last names in Korea are Kim, Lee, Park, Choi, and Chung, and account for almost 54 percent of the population's family name. Those with other last names are a minority of the population.

So it is more than likely to meet several "Mr. Kims" at a given

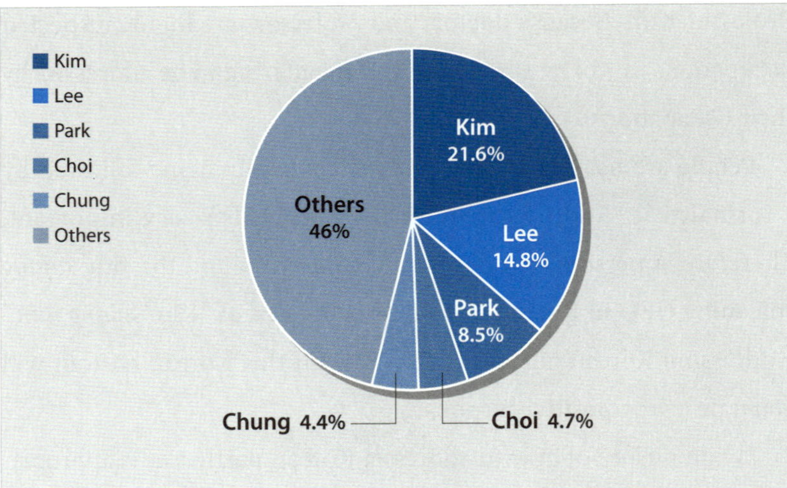

Figure 4-1 Korean family names (Korea National Statistical Office, 2000)

meeting. This is another reason to take good care of the business cards received in a meeting. In general, Westerners find it difficult to remember Asians' faces and vice-versa. Notes can be written on business cards to help remember certain physical features or unique characteristics of the newly acquainted. Such notes can prove to be very useful later on when trying to remember new acquaintances.

When a meeting is called, the highest ranking person will usually start with an opening statement. Beginning a meeting with the Korean greeting "*Annyeonghaseyo*? *Mannaseo bangapseumnida*." (Hello, it's a pleasure to meet you.) will leave the Koreans in the meeting with a strong, positive first impression. At the end of the meeting, the host party's leader will make a closing statement with another round of handshakes. At this time, usually the higher ranks will shake hands while the lower ranks will simply bow. After a particularly successful meeting, those who are familiar with Western culture may also exchange hugs.

Greetings of Different Countries

- **India:** Two hands are put together when greeting.
  * **Namaste:** Traditional Indian greeting that shows respect.
- **New Zealand Maori:** Noses touch when greeting each other.
- **Thailand:** The Wai, or putting one's hands together is the greatest sign of thanks.

  When a more senior person receives a Wai: Two hands are put together, but there is no bow.

  When greeting people of similar rank, fingertips are brought near the throat, but lower than the nose.

  When rank is not known, fingertips are brought near the throat, but lower than the nose.

  When a lower rank greets a higher-rank, the lower ranking person puts their hands together and bows their head while fingertips are placed at nose level.
- **Latin and Slavic Countries:** Hug and kiss on the cheeks.
- **Inuit:** Pats on the cheeks.
- **Tibet:** The ears are grabbed while the tongue is extended out.
- **Polynesian:** Noses are rubbed against one another.
- **Latin America:** The face is moved from side to side while embracing the other person.

Case Study

Differences in Culture

Mr. Kim is scheduled to pick up his Mexican business partner from the airport on Monday morning. Raul, the team leader from Mexico, meets Mr. Kim for the first time at the airport. As soon as Mr. Kim and Raul meet, Raul shakes hands and pats Mr. Kim's back several times as a greeting. The two begin to talk about Raul's time on the airplane. However, as the conversation goes on, Raul begins to speak closer and closer to Mr. Kim's face. Mr. Kim grows increasingly uncomfortable by this. As Raul continues talking, he congenially slaps Mr. Kim on the back as a sign of his growing sense of closeness with Mr. Kim. However, Mr. Kim finds this kind of physical contact uncomfortable. Finally, when they reach the hotel and Mr. Kim tells Raul that he will see him tomorrow, Raul pats Mr. Kim on the head and thanks him for picking him up from the airport. Mr. Kim is a little bewildered. How would you interpret what just happened?

Expert Opinion Mr. Kim experienced major cultural differences in his encounter with Raul. The concepts of personal space, respect, communication, and time are different between Mexico and Korea. Mr. Kim's bewilderment and perception of Raul as being rude were caused by these differences. It is common for Koreans to keep some physical space with someone they meet for the first time. Patting someone on the back or shoulders is often reserved only for very close friends. Patting someone on the head is considered something adults do to children, which could explain why Mr. Kim would think Raul is rude. However, all of this is due to cultural differences and any of these behaviors cannot be judged right or wrong. In this situation, Mr. Kim should try to understand the unique characteristics of Mexican culture and learn to accept the differences. Similarly, if Raul is going to continue doing business with Koreans, he will also have to learn about Korean culture and be mindful of it in his behavior.

Generally, meal times are avoided when scheduling meetings. However, if both parties are comfortable with the idea and the subject matter is not particularly serious, meetings over lunch or dinner are more than possible. If invited to a working lunch or dinner, this could be interpreted as a sign that the other party wants to reinforce the good relationship. Therefore, meal invitations should not be rejected unless there is a good reason.

Furthermore, many executives will take advantage of a breakfast meeting or a late dinner meeting to make use of their busy time. In some cases, weekend meetings can also be arranged and this is not an unusual practice for Korean businessmen. Should you happen to receive an invitation for a weekend meeting, feel free to graciously excuse yourself if you are not so inclined.

Case Study

Refusing a Mealtime Meeting

After smoothly closing a contract, Mark receives an invitation for dinner at the home of his Korean counterpart, Jinsoo Kim. Although Mark, an Englishman, is grateful for the invitation, he has a previous engagement and says that he will not be able to make it to the dinner. In fact, Mark cannot make it to Mr. Kim's invitation because the dinner is on his wedding anniversary and he has plans to celebrate the occasion with his wife. One week later, when Mark calls Mr. Kim to follow-up on the details of the contract, Mark feels that the conversation is not as friendly as before and, in fact, feels distance from Mr. Kim. Why did this happen? If you were Mark, what would you have done?

Expert Opinion Receiving an invitation to a meal is significant because for Koreans, doing business together means forming a relationship. Sharing a meal is an important aspect of this process and Koreans believe that it is a key to successful business. Of course, from Mark's perspective, he already had an appointment that he could not cancel. However, Mark should have at least explained his situation and asked if he could accept an invitation from Mr. Kim at another date. Had he done this, Mr. Kim would have understood that Mark was not refusing the invitation, but rather was unable to attend the event for good reason. However, there are some instances where prior engagements should be re-scheduled in order to accept an important business-related invitation.

3

Dress Code

As in other Asian countries, appearance is very important in Korea. Just as manners and etiquette are stressed, so is clothing, which was used to show one's rank and status in Korean society. Therefore, Koreans emphasize the importance of proper attire for the occasion.

Korean businessmen typically wear Western-style suits. An outfit usually consists of a dark suit, worn with a dress shirt and a tie. Since there are four distinct seasons in Korea, men wear seasonally appropriate suits. However, even during summer, it is usually not polite to remove one's jacket during a formal meeting. Also, wearing neckties are considered very polite and are not taken off for most occasions.

On the other hand, many companies today opt for a "business casual" dress code. The Korean government agencies also elected a no-tie dress code during the summer months. Obviously, dress codes can vary depending on the industry. The finance sector typically has more conservative dress code while in creativity-driven industries such as advertising or broadcasting agencies, dress code may not even be very important.

If unsure of dress code for a particular occasion, it is a good idea to ask your Korean counterpart what may be appropriate. If there is no way to find out what is appropriate beforehand, dressing at least business casual is probably the safest minimum standard. Being overdressed is usually better than being underdressed for any occasion.

Also, during hot weather or at restaurants, you will often find Korean businessmen asking if others would like to take off their jackets. This also signals the closeness in relationship, as one would not suggest so during a particularly formal meeting or with unfamiliar company. When asked to take off one's jacket, feel free to take up the offer or politely decline by saying "I will do so in a bit," if not inclined to do so.

What are dress codes like in other countries? In the UK, the Czech Republic, Vietnam, India, and Romania, for example, there are some variations in dress codes but unless at a special occasion, business casual for a business meeting is usually considered appropriate.

Case Study

Suit Jacket

Four members of a Korean team travel to Company A's headquarters in South Africa on a business trip. You are the person in charge of meetings. After the meeting, you, as the director of international affairs, are scheduled to lead the group on a tour. The weather is very hot and humid with the temperature outside rising to 30° C, or 86° F. As soon as you step outside, you feel the heat and immediately take off your jacket. However, your visitors from Asia continue to wear their jackets. Although you ask whether or not they would like to take off their jackets, they tell you that they are fine. What do you make of this situation?

Expert Opinion Korean business culture tends to be much more formal than in South Africa. While it is common to take off one's jacket during hot weather in Korea, the Koreans probably felt they must be courteous since they are visiting as guests. One possible solution to this situation would be to explain to the Korean guests that taking off one's jacket is not considered rude in South Africa. In general, it is important to follow the rules and etiquettes of the host country to ensure that everyone is comfortable and that the cultural distance can be minimized.

4

Korean Dining Etiquette

In general, Korean dining etiquette differs greatly from that of the West and is sometimes difficult for foreigners to follow. Eating unfamiliar foods using chopsticks may make dining in Korea an uncomfortable experience. However, learning about Korean dining culture can be an enjoyable and interesting experience.

First, let us start with entering the restaurant. It is important to remember the etiquette for Korean seating arrangements when sitting down in a restaurant. The higher rank person always sits down first. When given a choice, the junior person should always suggest that the senior person take the prime seats (as outlined before), preferably a seat away from the entrance and with a better view.

When the food arrives, it is important not to begin eating immediately. Instead, eating may begin when the most senior person picks up his or her utensils. The meal starts with everyone saying "bon appétit" (or in Korean, *Jal-meok-ge-sseum-ni-da*). In fact, saying "bon appétit," is also appropriate and not uncommon at all among Korean businessmen.

One may notice that there is a large population of Christians,

Catholics and Buddhists in Korea who pray before meals. As we learned in Chapter 1, Koreans are known to have strong, religious beliefs. Furthermore, one should be careful not to eat noisily. Talking with one's mouth full is frowned upon, as in many other countries. Traditionally, Koreans thought it was polite to eat silently. Perhaps this is why Koreans tend to not talk much and rush through meals. Regardless, this is why many Koreans find it difficult to have long conversations during mealtime. Moreover, most Koreans are not used to having to wait between courses. Korean cuisine is typically served all at once, although some Korean restaurants serve food in courses. Even so, the interval between each course is much shorter than in Western cuisine. Westerners may find it surprising that dishes are served so quickly.

In general, spoons and chopsticks are not held together in one hand. Also, it is important not to leave the spoon sitting in the rice bowl. This is traditionally reserved for Korean *jesa* ceremonies honoring the deceased. When not in use, utensils should be placed neatly next to one's plate or bowl. Soup should be eaten without holding the bowl and rice should be eaten from one side of the bowl. Eating with bowls and plates held up is frowned upon in Korea. Traditionally, only beggars would hold up their bowls when eating, which in turn became a sign of being low class. On the contrary, Japanese thought that only animals would leave their bowls on the ground and therefore dine holding the bowls in their hands. It is easy to see that even between neighboring countries, dining etiquettes can differ widely.

When dining, it is usually customary to keep the pace of the most senior person in a group and agree to leave when the most senior person finishes eating and suggests so. When Korean people leave the dining table, most will say, "Thank you for the meal." or (in Korean, *Jal- meo-geo-sseum-ni-da*) as a sign of respect and appreciation.

Now, let us turn to dining etiquette in other cultures. In Western dining etiquette, fruits, breads and meats are should be cut into bite-size pieces before eating. Meat is cut using a knife in the right hand and a fork in the left. After the meat is cut into a bite-size piece, the knife is put down, but if the fork is moved to the right hand to eat this is considered to be bad manners, except in America. Other types of food, like pizza, are traditionally eaten by hand without utensils.

A unique practice when dining in China is that an even number of dishes is ordered. In Chinese culture, even numbers are generally considered better than odd numbers. Accordingly, they normally invite an even number of guests. Chinese restaurants typically have tables with lazy susans in the center (rotating center). This allows food to be easily shared around the table. It is important to remember that lazy susans should only be rotated clockwise.

In India, food is often eaten with the hands. Because the left hand is considered dirtier of the two hands, most food is eaten exclusively with the right hand. In more upscale restaurants, fingerbowls are provided for customers to wash their hands before eating. Lemon juice is sometimes added to the water in fingerbowls as well. However, although most food is eaten with the hands, food that is too hot is sometimes eaten with a wooden spoon. In general, conversation is avoided during a meal in India. Instead, conversation usually begins after the meal when both the hands and the mouth have been wiped clean.

5
Business Entertainment

Koreans are generally very good at entertaining guests. In fact, Korea is well known for treating guests with good hospitality. This can be attributed to Korea's nomadic roots. Nomadic tribes are historically known to extend warm hospitality to guests coming from a great distance. This is because such guests coming from afar often brought vital information that helped the otherwise secluded, nomadic tribes survive. So Koreans typically never send a guest home unhappy. As we learned in Chapter 1, the idea of sending a guest home happy is also related to the "face saving" culture in Korea.

Regardless of how much a person might dislike another, the general rule in Korea is that a guest in one's home should be treated with the best hospitality. Doing so would be the honorable thing to do for a respectable host. However, receiving hospitality from a Korean does not necessarily mean that one can achieve success in business. As mentioned, hospitality and business are two different things to Koreans.

Koreans typically feel obligated to take care of their guests for the entire duration of their stay. This usually includes meals, arranging for transportation as well as recreational activities. This amount of attention can be overwhelming for some foreigners. If a foreign guest is taken to a restaurant with a Korean host, it is common for the host to treat their visitor to a meal. Unfortunately this can be unsettling for foreigner who may feel indebted to a stranger. However, this should be interpreted as an attempt to extend good hospitality to the guests so it should be well received.

Although it was more common for Koreans to invite foreign partners to their homes in the past, the rise of the nuclear families, along with smaller living spaces in apartments, have made home visits less common today. However, one should not miss an opportunity to visit a Korean home if invited. These visits are usually marked by the same warm atmosphere commonly felt at housewarming parties and are no doubt unique experiences.

When invited to a home, small gifts like wine, fruit baskets and thank-you letters are usually considered polite. Large or expensive gifts are often burdensome for hosts to receive. We will elaborate more on this topic when we discuss gift giving later in this chapter.

In Korea, Dutch paying is not a familiar concept. Instead, it is customary for individuals to take turns in paying for the entire meal. That is, Koreans are not used to standing in front of the cashier, trying to figure out how much each person needs to pay. If a Korean insists they pay for the entire meal, there is no need to be surprised. You can pay for the meal next time. In such instances, saying "I will buy next time," or "I will treat you when you visit my country," would be appropriate. Generally, it is common for higher ranks to pay for the meal, but when the meal is paid for by the company, you will often find that lower ranks will pay using the company credit card. However, in personal settings, seniors are usually expected to pay for the meal.

One enjoyable aspect of working with Koreans is the "*Hoesik*" culture, which are after-work parties with drinks. *Hoesik* usually takes place by departments or teams. They will leave the office together for dinner followed by drinks. *Hoesik* is used to build teamwork and foster group communication. *Hoesik* is also used to reward the successes and motivate the employees. While the frequency of *hoesik* varies by each company's budget and culture, one *hoesik* per month is typical.

Conversations at a *hoesik* tend to be more informal and personal than at the office, which makes it useful for personal networking and sharing information. It is a good idea to attend a *hoesik* at least once for the sake of experience. If unable to attend a *hoesik* of one's workgroup, letting coworkers know in advance will excuse the absence without damaging the overall group spirit.

Korea has one of the highest alcohol consumption rates per capita in the world. This is partly because most business meetings involve large amounts of alcohol. Of course, if someone does not want to drink, no one would be forced to do so. However, there is a general perception that by eating and drinking together, people can develop stronger bonds. Nevertheless, most Koreans understand if one does not drink or drink very little for health or religious reasons.

The overall Korean drinking culture is conducive to drinking in large quantities. Korean men tend to think that drinking a lot is very masculine, which often leads to excessive drinking. Therefore, people will continue to offer drinks. However, if one cannot drink or prefer not to, one can always respectfully decline. Even if one does not drink, it is usually a good idea to raise a full glass of an alcoholic beverage and say "cheers" (*geonbae* in Korean) with others. This is a symbolic gesture that wishes for the successful future, even though it literally means to "empty the glass."

Do other countries have a *hoesik* cultures similar to Korea's? In countries like the UK, Romania, the Czech Republic and India, there is not as strong a *hoesik* culture but there are still some similarities. However, Vietnamese workers often get together to eat and go for drinks. As we learned in Chapter 2, this could be attributed to the group mentality of Eastern countries as opposed to the more individualistic cultures of Western countries. Westerners view corporations as a streamlined system designed to efficiently manage given tasks and functions. On the other hand, corporations are seen as a group where people work together in the East. In the East, employees and companies are socially bound to another and a corporation's functions and its performance is influenced by these relationships.

6

Gift Giving

Giving gifts is always a fun activity. Gifting expresses the desire for a good relationship as well as reciprocation of the affection received. However, as in many other countries, extravagant gifts can be considered as bribes and make the recipient uncomfortable. Gifts do not have to be expensive so long as it shows thoughtfulness. Often times, items representative of one's company, country or region make good gifts. Alternatively, gifts can also be given to the recipients' family members, such as spouses or children and shows further thoughtfulness and consideration.

Some people like to give smaller gifts often. Some even bring gifts to a dinner. In such cases, smaller, affordable gifts under $10 would be appropriate. A gift costing more than $20 to $30 may be considered too expensive and make the receiver uncomfortable. However, gifts that are regional specialties may exceed these general price guidelines and still be well accepted. It is important to keep in mind the differences in cultural norms when considering appropriate gifts.

Let us take a look at gift-giving cultures in other countries. In countries like the UK, the Czech Republic, Vietnam, India, and Romania, gift giving is generally modest and similar to exchanging souvenirs. Therefore, giving expensive gifts in these countries is usually seen as outside the norm.

What are some culturally insensitive or inappropriate gifts? While gift giving is fun for both givers and receivers, differences in culture may cause unexpected faux pas. In the United States, lilies are often used in funerals and not generally gifted to others. Likewise, a cake is usually an inappropriate gift when going to someone's home because many hostesses will prepare their own cake. In Europe, flowers are not usually given as gifts in even numbers. The number thirteen is also considered unlucky in Europe, therefore a bouquet of thirteen flowers is also not given as a gift. On the other hand, the number four represents death in many Asian cultures so bouquets of four flowers are usually avoided.

The Chinese generally stay away from giving grandfather clocks as gifts because the gong sound is associated with death. Umbrellas should also be avoided because the word umbrella also means the "end of a relationship." Chinese people tend to prefer even numbers over odd numbers because odd numbers are traditionally seen as unlucky. Therefore, Chinese monetary gifts will usually come in even-number amounts for celebratory occasions and odd-number amounts of a sombre occasion. It should be noted that because Chinese consider it courteous to reject a gift at least three times, it is important to offer gifts several times.

In Japan, a knife represents the severing ties and is usually avoided as a gift. Flowers are given in odd numbers when offered as gifts. Similarly, Koreans prefer odd numbers because it represents positive energy in Confucian tradition. Flowers as well as monetary gifts for celebratory occasions such as weddings and birthdays, are usually given in odd numbers. Their favorite number is 3.

In Islamic cultures, a gift of pork or an alcoholic beverage is a major faux pas since they are forbidden by the Koran. Products made from pigskin or alcohol, such as perfume, can also be considered insensitive and discourteous by the Muslims.

7

Cultural Differences and Misunderstandings

Misunderstanding could take place between foreigners and Koreans due to different cultures and customs. Some behaviors considered kind to Koreans could be impolite to foreigners.

What are some common misunderstandings about Korean behaviors? Typically when Koreans are reprimanded, they do not make eye contact because it is not polite. However, for Westerners, eye contact is very important in such situations. Westerners typically see such lack of eye contact as a sign of disrespect and dishonesty. Also, when reprimanded, a Korean may not respond to questioning simply because answering questions can be seen as talking back to seniors and will be seen as rude.

Another frequently misunderstood Korean behavior is holding hands or interlocking arms with close friends of the same gender. This is especially common among Korean women. Koreans often do this purely as a demonstration of their close friendship however many Westerners mistake this as homosexuality. Likewise, when Korean businessmen travel overseas, they often share hotel rooms with others of the same gender. Although this may appear strange to many Westerners, there is nothing strange about this to Koreans. When Korea was less economically developed, Korean businessmen often shared hotel rooms with their coworkers to lower travel expenses. As a result, room sharing still remains a part of Korean corporate culture to this day. Moreover, Koreans are very used to sharing rooms in general because Korean families have traditionally lived together in extended families and sharing rooms was customary.

In fact, some Koreans may never have had their own rooms their entire lives. From childhood through marriage, some people constantly share rooms with family members. Yet, because of Korea's recent economic development, the concept of the nuclear family has made Koreans increasingly independent. The sizes of families have decreased and the children in most Korean households today no longer share rooms with their siblings.

Another commonly misunderstood custom is sharing glasses when drinking. Koreans will often share glasses as a sign of true friendship. On the other hand, Westerners are taught from a very early age that sharing glasses with others is not hygienic. Increasing awareness in hygiene has changed some of these practices in Korea. For example, when drink glasses are shared, they are usually cleaned with a tissue before being passed on to the next person.

There are also behaviors that Koreans could misunderstand about foreigners. Westerners often use their index fingers to point to people or objects to draw attention. Unfortunately, pointing fingers is considered very rude and Koreans will often use other objects such as pens to point to a person or an object.

Also, blowing one's nose at the table during meals is considered rude in Korea. On the other hand, Koreans are often more generous than Westerners when it comes to burping. In Korea, burping has traditionally been a way of showing one's appreciation for food at a meal. Although public burping is not so common now, this behavior is usually not seen as rude.

Westerners generally give and receive things with one hand even with elders. To Koreans this is seen as very rude because in Korea, everything is given and received with two hands. This is especially so when giving and receiving from elders and demonstrates respect to others, particularly to those who are older.

Finally, Koreans do not like to write their names in red ink because red ink is used to write the name of the dead. However, the color of the ink has little or no significance to many Westerners.

Summary of Chapter 4

1. Making an Appointment

- Typically, Koreans schedule appointments at least two weeks in advance.
- If temporarily visiting Korea on business, it is more than likely that one will be able to schedule meeting within one week of initiating contact.
- With close relationships, informal channels can be used to arrange a meeting. If the meeting is mutually very important, appointments can be scheduled on weekends or holidays.
- In general, it is recommended one schedules a meeting and be introduced through a mutual acquaintance.

2 Meetings

- Koreans typically introduce themselves in hierarchical order, starting with the higher rank to lower and older to younger. Therefore, when introducing one's party, it is advisable to do same.

3. Dress Code

- Like other Asian countries that stress formality, appearance is very important in Korea. Clothing traditionally served as the tool to indicate rank and status in Korean society. Therefore, Koreans highly value proper attire for any occasion.
- Many companies today opt for the business casual dress code.

4. Korean Dining Etiquette

- It is important to not begin eating right away and wait until the highest ranking person picks up their utensils. The meal starts by saying "bon appétit" (or in Korean, *Jal-meok-ge-sseum-ni-da*).

5. Business Entertainment

- Koreans are renowned for their warm hospitality to their guests. Such hospitality to guests should be understood as their desire and effort to build a good relationship and should be well received.
- One enjoyable aspect of working with Koreans is the "*Hoesik*" culture.
- *Hoesik* is used for building teamwork and is used to help facilitate communication.

6. Gift Giving

- Giving gifts expresses the desire for a good relationship as well as returning affection.
- However, as in many other countries, extravagant gifts can be considered as bribes and make the recipient uncomfortable. Gifts do not have to be expensive as long as it shows thoughtfulness.

7. Cultural Differences and Misunderstandings

- There are many common misunderstandings that arise from cultural differences.
- Understanding the cultural differences and applying them to daily life will be helpful in building good relationships with those from other cultures.

Chapter 05

Communication and Negotiation

1 Communication

2 Characteristics of Koreans and Korean Groups Concerning Communication

3 Features of Korean Communication

4 Negotiation

1

Communication

In this chapter, we will take a look at communication, specifically Koreans' general communication styles. We will also discuss how Koreans negotiate.

First, let us define communication. Communication is the process of two or more people conveying a variety of opinions and emotions verbally and nonverbally to produce mutual understanding. Communication is a two-way street between individuals or groups to derive a common ground or understandings. Thus, simple explanations, instructions or any other unilateral communication cannot be viewed as true and meaningful communication.

In a business environment, communication is an action taken to share information between individuals and departments to make decisions and execute tasks efficiently. Orders and instructions are other forms of communication used by senior managers to manage subordinates by setting clear work guidelines and job expectations. Companies use communication as a tool to boost employees' morale through praising performances and achievements and to allow employees to express their satisfaction, dissatisfaction, and enthusiasm to coworkers, superiors as well as to those outside of the organization. Various types of communication connect each individual and sub-units in the company together.

Next, let us take a look at the different types of communication in an organization. Typically, information flows within established channels of the organization. These channels are called networks and greatly influence the organization and its members' behaviors and performances. We can categorize the types of communication into the following:

1. Top-down/Bottom-up Communication
2. Horizontal/Vertical Communication
3. Individual/Group Communication
4. Internal/External Communication

Top-down Communication typically originates from top managers that are concerned with the general well-being of the organization. However, businesses that lean excessively towards this approach rely heavily on the decisions of its senior managers. Consequently, employee ideas and work autonomy are restricted, making it easy for the firm to become increasingly inefficient and resistant to change.

Horizontal Communication refers to communication between organizational members of the same hierarchical rank. Organizations that facilitate flexible communication between members of different ranks by appropriately delegating responsibility also actively utilize Horizontal Communication. Typically, informal communication travels horizontally, rather than vertically. Vertical Communication is generally more top-down, such as relaying a directive by the executive management.

Communication between coworkers is considered Individual Communication while communication between unions and management or between sales and marketing teams is defined as Group

Communication. Individual Communication occurs when two or more individuals exchange individual work-related information or build personal relationships. These personal communications may not be directly related to the organizations' goals but may have indirect influence by affecting personal relationships. Group Communication often helps to mediate conflicts and increase performance efficiency through the exchange of information among sub-groups.

Lastly, communication within an organization as it relates to work, such as between managers, is called Internal Communication. External Communication involves an audience external to the organization such as suppliers, service providers, clients and the general public. Advertisements and public relations are also considered External Communication.

Communication can be either verbal or nonverbal. Using both forms of communication together reinforces each other and tends to be more effective. Historically, communication only referred to verbal communication, but recent research points to the importance of nonverbal communication in effective communication. Nonverbal communication such as body language can be extremely useful in facilitating smooth communication in the presence of a language barrier.

2

Characteristics of Koreans and Korean Groups Concerning Communication

To understand how Koreans communicate, let us learn about how Koreans and Korean organizations communicate.

Koreans tend to keep their distance before they establish personal relationships. However, once someone is accepted as a member of their group, newcomers are quickly assimilated into the spirit of the workplace. Koreans also shy away from sharing information about themselves before getting to know the other person. They are typically very cautious and shy with strangers, but once a relationship is forged through a casual round of *soju* (Korean distilled beverage), they will quickly become very open and affectionate. An old Korean adage says close friends know the number of pieces of silverware in a friend's home, illustrating how common it is for Koreans to share intimate details with their friends. This is largely different from the West, where even close friends may not share very personal information. You will recall the differences that we covered in Chapter 2 concerning relationships with Koreans.

Koreans often identify themselves as members of groups. That is, Koreans have a strong sense of belonging to a group and sometimes they sacrifice their individual interests for the group. This is more pronounced in smaller groups. Remember that Koreans have a tendency toward small-group collectivism. These organizations typically value good cooperation and not imposing personal opinions. Like the famous dish *bibimbap* we saw in Chapter 3, Koreans believe that mixing with others and living in harmony creates a positive synergy.

Self-sacrifice and loyalty are commonly emphasized in Korean organizations. Many job interviews will ask, "In what ways are you ready to make sacrifices for the company?" In Korean companies, it is difficult for employees to leave work before others, even at late hours. Doing so would usually be perceived as being overwhelmingly individualistic and lacking in camaraderie. Leaving before your boss will be seen likewise and helping busy coworkers are generally expected.

The same is true when a more senior employee remains in the office. It is natural for that person to expect help from others when working late. Thus for many Koreans, personal sacrifice in organizations is very logical. Koreans believe that making personal sacrifice demonstrates their faithful attitude towards their organization and expect the organization to do the same. However, this is less and less likely with younger generations that are increasingly individualistic. This is indicative of westernization in Korea.

Traditionally, Koreans have been more relationship-oriented than task-oriented in their decision-making and prioritized loyalty and responsibility. As a result, refusing superior's orders is difficult in Korea. However, this is also changing with the advent of individualism and rising awareness in maintaining healthy organizational culture. Many younger generations prefer not to participate in company outings and would rather join small interest groups. They also prefer to avoid heavy drinking at *hoesik*.

Do Koreans like to compete or cooperate in their work? Individual accomplishments and success are important to Koreans. However, Koreans will also assign great value to working harmoniously with their colleagues. A person who focuses more on individual accomplishments may create conflict within the group and receive poor evaluation as a team player. Moreover, Korean corporations like to encourage a family-like working environment, although this may vary depending on the industry, gender ratio, and the organizational culture. Investment firms, for example, are typically more competitive and male-dominated than other industries. Nevertheless, emphasis on cooperative relationships amongst colleagues is considered to be the norm.

Koreans do not like uncertainty and will often try to minimize unpredictable factors in any situation. Generally they are risk averse and prefer clearly defined variables and guidelines for a task. However this does not mean that Koreans will always abide by these guidelines. Korean employees seek clearly defined roles and responsibilities to reduce confusion and believe that this increases work efficiency. They also tend to perform better when they clearly understand their evaluation criteria. However, even when roles are clearly defined, they will often seek and give help to their coworkers when the workload increases. Koreans in general do not want the demands of their tasks to exceed their responsibilities and sometimes have difficulty getting started when not given specific directions or guidelines. Overall they tend to perform better in a structured environment.

However, Korean corporations increasingly emphasize creativity and innovation, urging their employees to think outside the box and adapt to the rapidly changing management environments of today.

Case Study

Koreans Want Defined Guidelines

You are a manager from the Czech Republic who just held a meeting with the Human Resources (HR) team on the implementation of a new performance management program. During the meeting, the HR director did not provide clear answers to the many questions brought to the table. Instead of setting clear guidelines, the director suggested flexible adaptation to the changing environment and wanted further discussion to decide on the future direction of the program. While you were satisfied with these results and thought it was a productive meeting, your Korean colleague said it was a very unproductive and disappointing meeting. He criticized that the HR director was underprepared and could not provide clear guidelines to the team. Why were the two assessments different?

Expert Opinion As explained, Koreans do not like uncertainty. They try to minimize unpredictability and prefer their superiors to set clear guidelines for their tasks. They also perform better when their tasks and roles are clearly defined. Moreover, it is customary for Koreans to privately caucus on what is on the agenda prior to meetings. For Koreans, meetings are not for discussion but rather for making decisions. Therefore, those who cannot provide sufficient answers to questions are seen as underprepared. On the other hand, Western organizational culture favors active discussions during meetings and prefers arriving at solutions based on everyone's opinion. Because active discussions are often accompanied by some disagreement, multiple meetings may be expected in order to reach a decision.

On the other hand, Koreans are very good at adapting to their environments. Many Korean corporations do not have detailed job descriptions so employees often have to work as situations arise, which is not typically accepted in other cultures. So let us take a look at how others cultures deal with this.

In most cultures, workers are not very willing to accept additional task beyond their job descriptions. In Britain, such requests are considered absurd and not well accepted unless it makes logical sense. Similarly, in the Czech Republic, Vietnam and Romania, tasks beyond job descriptions are received negatively. Indians are slightly less negative about these tasks and will accept with reservation if assigned by a superior.

In contrast, Koreans are generally very accepting of tasks beyond their job description as long as they are assigned by their superiors. If a Korean supervisor or manager assigns a task not included in the employee's job description, it is often better to resolve the problem through direct communication. If one only does work included in their job description, they may be viewed as holding back the overall group's momentum and progress. Therefore, cooperation is necessary for the overall success of the organization.

Traditionally, Koreans process information by looking at the big picture as a sum of individual parts. That is, Koreans tend to see a task in its entirety instead of individual pieces. However, business processes often require a more linear approach. You may want to recall the differences in Eastern and Western ways of thinking that we discussed earlier.

Koreans also tend to use a similar approach in evaluating performance. Evaluations include not only individual goals but also his or her diligence and relationships with others. This type of performance is rooted in the tendency to prefer the "big picture." In contrast, younger Koreans are generally less interested in the big picture and tend to focus on their specific tasks. Korean companies are also increasingly asking their employees to take a step-by-step approach to their work.

3
Features of Korean Communication

One should keep in mind that Koreans often do not say everything they want to express. Koreans rely on different tone of voice, facial expressions, context, and how they start the conversation to fully express their message.

"*Nunchi*" literally means "measurement of the eye," which is a Korean word for the ability to quickly and accurately sense the other party's intention. Although there is no direct translation for *nunchi*, it can be roughly translated as a keen sense of understanding others' moods and intentions. Because Koreans use much nonverbal communication, *nunchi* is very important in understanding Koreans' true intentions when they speak. Koreans often speak indirectly and often don't express their likes or dislikes explicitly, which requires good *nunchi* to correctly interpret the situation.

If one cannot accurately grasp other people's intentions in conversations, they are deemed "*nunchi*less." Also, when one cannot get a good read on a particular situation and behave inappropriately, they are considered to be without *nunchi*. Does this make sense? Let us take a look at the following to help understand this concept. Try to guess who does and does not have *nunchi* in each situation.

It is time for a weekly Thursday meeting. Five out of six people are on time, but Mr. Kim has not arrived yet. The team leader does not refer directly to Mr. Kim but talks about the importance of the weekly meetings and punctuality. At that moment, Mr. Kim opens the door wide and makes a leisurely entrance with a big smile on his face and Starbucks takeout cup in his hand. Everyone looks at Mr. Kim. Mr. Kim sits down noisily and asks a colleague next to him, "What's going on today? Something feels a little strange." Here, Mr. Kim was late but tactlessly failed to sense the general atmosphere of the meeting and made others feel uncomfortable. And yet, he is still smiling!

Here is another example of a person without *nunchi*. It's almost 7 pm and manager Kim asks assistant manager Choi if he can stay with him to work late tonight. Assistant manager Choi's facial expression clearly shows discomfort and he answers "yes" in a small voice without conviction. In fact, assistant manager Choi had made plans to see his girlfriend that evening, but he could not refuse his superior's request. Manager Kim says to him, "Assistant manager Choi, you are the only one I can count on. I knew you'd be happy to help me out." If manager Kim had *nunchi*, he would have been able to catch assistant manager Choi' awkward facial expression. Had he seen this, he would have asked if assistant manager Choi had plans for the evening and if it was something he could reschedule. If not, assistant manager Choi could have looked for an alternative.

Of course, Koreans typically do not expect foreigners to have *nunchi*. As a result, they will often try to be explicit and direct in their communication with foreigners. This style of communication is not often used and the language barrier may make the dialogue sound impolite than intended to foreigners. Please note that this is not because of their lack of manners but only because they wish to be clear in their communication.

Similarly, top-down communications and directives are sometimes not clearly delivered because of a lack of explicit communication. In such cases, subordinates will seek information through various other channels. When a lack of communication results in subpar performance, many will point fingers to who is responsible. Strangely, even in these situations, indirect communication is preferred.

In a similar vein, Koreans do not like confrontation when conflicts arise. They prefer to resolve their conflicts implicitly because they do not like to speak directly about the "harsh truth." When asked for feedback, they will more than likely give positive comments. If you want what they really think, it is the best to ask for specific responses to detailed questions.

For example, rather than asking, "Do you like this plan?" or "What do you think about this plan?" asking specific questions like, "What do you think needs improvement in this plan?" will be helpful. When Koreans want to disagree, they may say, "I will think about it," or "I'll need some time to make a decision." Misunderstanding such comments as positive feedback can cause conflicts in the future.

Indirect communication is another way Koreans "save face" and avoid conflicts. They generally believe that direct conflict may be taken personally and cause one to lose face in front of others. Therefore, Koreans may avoid direct conflict resolution and prefer to resolve conflicts in private. For example, when a team falls short of its monthly goal, the manager may imply that the team should work harder next month rather than pointing out that they fell short for that month. Likewise, if a team member is constantly late, the manager would comment on the team's work ethic. The same is true when Koreans achieve a goal or are successful. They will often not celebrate outright, but say something like "We did our best and fortunately got good results, but we could have done better," to maintain humble appearance.

Case Study

Indirect Expression

Joseph Dalton is a British employee in charge of the Asia-Pacific regional marketing at your office. He recently went to Korea on a business trip and negotiated with a Korean vendor. In order to supply the factories in the Asia-Pacific region with an 8 percent price reduction in parts, he needed to receive a price reduction confirmation from the Korean vendor. During the negotiations, the Korean vendor nodded his head, kept silent for a while and said, "I understand. I will do my best." After Joseph returned to Australia, he asked the Korean vendor for a written price quote reflecting the reduced price, but still had not received any response after two weeks. If you were Joseph, how would you interpret this situation and what would you do?

Expert Opinion Koreans tend to communicate indirectly to keep up appearances and to avoid conflicts in communication. At the time, the Korean vendor was trying to be considerate, so he looked away and gave a vague answer. This response was supposed to indicate that he would most likely not accept the offer. The reason the Korean vendor did not clearly reject Joseph's request was in order to avoid being impolite and avoid cutting off negotiations. By asking for more time, he was implying that he would like to further negotiate the price reduction. If Joseph hopes to maintain a good relationship with the vendor, he should probably contact the vendor again and reduce his demands or suggest an additional incentive.

Let us examine how other countries communicate. The British also have a tendency to be implicit and indirect in their communication, however in Vietnam, Romania, and India, communication is much more direct in business settings.

Now, let us take a look at communication patterns within an organization. The Korean culture of valuing formality is also manifested in intra-organizational communications. Communications within an organization often use appropriate honorific expressions according to age and rank, and show respect. Even though some companies encourage informal communication to create a familial and liberal work environment, in the presence of outsiders, formal conversations are encouraged. When conversing with older or higher-ranking managers, juniors tend to listen while their older superiors lead the conversations.

As discussed in Chapters 1 and 3, discussion can be difficult between ranks in Korea's hierarchical culture. Rather, they prefer to listen to their superiors. When Koreans have an opinion, they prefer to have a private caucus before or after the meeting or informally after work during *hoesik*. This is largely to prevent possible confusion and embarrassment for their superiors by bringing up unexpected topics in front of others.

Multinational organizations on the other hand, typically value active discussions. Those who are not fluent in English find it difficult to get involved in the conversation, so they typically listen more than they speak. In such cases, it would be considerate for fluent English speakers to take breaks, confirm everyone has understood and allow time for comprehension.

One will often find that Koreans engage in private conversations in Korean during meetings. This can be perceived as rude and disturbing to other attendees at the meeting. However, these private conversations are often to help their colleagues with English comprehension and should not be taken as offensive. Moreover, some Koreans will say "yes" to save face or to not disrupt the flow of the meeting even when they do not fully understand the issue at hand. If it seems that Korean attendees have difficulty understanding the meeting agenda, it is a good idea to take a break and suggest that someone explain.

Case Study

Language Barrier Issues

Minsoo Lee, a Korean man, told a Czech man named Mirka angrily that he was very unhappy with a meeting that he had had with a group of foreigners. He complained to Mirka that people from the UK and Australia did not understand how hard it was for non-native English speakers to understand and speak English. Some of the foreigners did not bother to explain and simply demanded their requests. People like Minsoo were obviously very startled to find themselves in such a situation. Why did Minsoo feel so frustrated?

Expert Opinion Minsoo was disappointed when he felt that his native English-speaking colleagues were not adequately considerate of the non-native speakers. When all attendees are from the same culture and speak the same language, all types of communication are easily understood. However this is not the case in this meeting and Minsoo is used to indirect conversation and communication, which are common in Korean culture.

Minsoo's foreign colleagues should be mindful of their non-native English speaking counterparts. It is important to always check when speaking with non-native speakers to ensure that everything is being communicated clearly.

As previously mentioned, Koreans are not used to explicitly saying "no." This is particularly confusing when questions are asked in the negative form. For example, when asked "Don't you like rainy days?" one would answer in English, "No, I don't." In Korean however, the answer to such a question is "yes," meaning, "You're right. I don't like rainy days." Therefore, it is better to ask Koreans these questions in a positive form instead of negative to avoid confusion, such as, "Do you dislike rainy days?" or, "Did you miss the meeting?" instead of, "Didn't you go to the meeting?"

It is also a good idea to confirm the other person's response when it is unclear if he or she correctly understood the question. For example, confirming with a follow up question such as "You mean you don't like rainy days?" would be helpful in clarifying what the speaker intended to say. This is a common mistake among even fluent English-speaking Koreans.

Now, let us address misunderstandings that may arise from a lack of vocabulary. For example, Koreans typically have difficulty with auxiliary verbs such as should, have to, can, and may. This is because many cannot distinguish between the subtle nuances of these verbs. If the auxiliary "should" is used in place of "can," foreigners may feel that the speaker is being demanding. However for Koreans, the word "should" is often misused to express something strongly. (Instead of saying, "You can take off your jacket," they would say, "You should take off your jacket.")

Most Koreans are also unfamiliar with British English because American English is taught in the Korean educational system. The different pronunciation between American and British English is often very tough for Koreans to understand. Also, there are differences in vocabulary between American and British English. To give just a few examples:

"Sidewalk" in American English is "pavement" in British English.
"Subway" in American English is "underground" in British English.
"Takeout" in American English is "takeaway" in British English.
"Check," at a restaurant in American English, is "bill" in British English.
"Elevator" in American English is "lift" in British English.

In addition to language barriers and cultural differences, there are many difficult situations that require clear communication in terms of language and expressions. This is particularly true in business meetings. It is always better to use language that non-native speakers can understand easily, speak clearly and simply, and repeat. It is a good idea to ask questions during conversations to confirm the other party's understanding. Also, it may be more efficient to explain relevant content with charts or distribute printed summaries beforehand. It may also help to exchange meeting memos to make sure everyone has an accurate understanding of what was discussed in the meeting. Quick summaries after each item on the meeting agenda will also help non-native speakers engage more during meetings. Of course this type of communication requires more time and preparation, but it will reduce miscommunication and ultimately increase efficiency.

We learned that Koreans are cautious about expressing their opinions in front of others. This is because Koreans often worry about whether they are being reasonable or not and whether their opinions will hurt someone's feelings. Especially, they like to give only positive, superficial feedback in public because they worry that their feedbacks may be taken personally. In a relation-oriented society, everything can be taken personally, so Koreans tend to be careful about reading others' feelings and try to avoid offending others. Furthermore, Koreans are usually slow to respond to questions and many would rather wait for others' response, which can become hindrance in active exchange of ideas.

Work and personal relationships are often not clearly defined in Korea. Those with personal ties such as same educational background may be subjected to more complicated etiquette. For example, one's senior alumnus should always be treated as one's senior in the workplace. However alumnus relationships are typically difficult to maintain between younger upperclassmen and older underclassmen.

As we learned earlier, Koreans are averse to conflicts and arguments. They are collectivistic, hierarchical and are used to receiving superior's demands, so differences in opinion are usually not welcomed. The tendency to avoid conflict and emphasis on harmony in relationships is rooted in their culture. Preference for indirection and formality in communication is also a testament to their aversion to conflict.

How Meetings Are Conducted

Some meetings are scheduled in advance and some are last minute. Meetings scheduled in advance tend to have a specific agenda or serve as town hall meetings. Either way, attendees are usually notified of the meeting agenda via email and they are often sent reminders if the meeting is important. Most meetings are attended by external guests or many attendees.

On the other hand, internal meetings can be held last minute, or at the request of senior management. These are usually to deliver specific instructions or to follow-up on an ongoing task.

When arranging meetings with foreigners, it is important for Koreans to clearly define the nature of the meeting, whether it is a discussion, a kick off meeting for a new project, or a performance evaluation. It is also important to understand the attendee's intention and attitude about the meeting agenda prior to the meeting.

4

Negotiation

First, let us review the general concept of negotiations. Negotiations are attempts to reach mutually agreed settlements between different parties with varying opinions. Whether the differences in opinion is the sale price of a home, work contract, salaries, or diplomatic relations, negotiations are typically used to resolve differences. We also negotiate in our daily lives; for instance, every parent can probably recall negotiating with their children on reducing the time spent playing video games.

Negotiations are even more entrenched in today's business processes. Negotiations usually begin with the exchange of business cards along with formal greetings and introductions. Informal small talk usually follows. Typically, Koreans are interested in who their counterparts are, but since they also prefer quick business deals they usually do not spend too much time on small talk. When things get rough during negotiation, they will usually ask for a short break.

Depending on who is at the negotiating table, decision-making time may vary. In the past, only the leader of the organization had decision-making authority, but these days some of the decision-making authority is delegated to the negotiators. Nevertheless, senior managers reserve the authority to make decisions on important matters. Financial matters, such as those related to expenses and prices, are considered the most important. Koreans tend to deal with finances at the beginning of the negotiations when they are buyers and in the final stages when they are sellers.

Koreans regard the signing of a contract as the beginning of a formal relationship and will often try to maintain a good relationship. They will often assume that the terms of a contract can be renegotiated under new circumstances and likewise, are often generous in accepting renegotiation at the other party's request. However, Westerners see a contract as a legally binding document once it is signed. Therefore, it is a good idea to remember that Koreans consider contractual relations to be long-term and aim for win-win situations for both parties.

Failure in negotiations creates many problems in a culture that is hierarchy-oriented. Most do not want to take the risk of responsibility of failure unless they have full authority to control the situation.

However, some are more than willing to take risks with the quintessentially Korean "can do" or "never fail" spirit.

The time required to conclude negotiations is influenced by various factors, depending on the situation. It may take longer to work towards an agreement because all individuals in an organization value consensus. It takes more time to make decisions when an issue is very important and many interested parties are involved, because all stakeholders will review the case.

Let us take a look at some business negotiations. For instance, let us assume that you are a used car salesman. You are currently negotiating the price of a car with a particularly picky customer. Your purchase price for the car was $10,000 and your current selling price is $13,000. The customer is offering $11,000. How would you negotiate in this situation?

Step 1: Opening the Negotiations

A smooth opening can lead to successful negotiation. Therefore, it is important to break the ice as you start the negotiation by building rapport through finding common ground. You can then make your first offer. Most people would rather hear the other sides' offer first. This is usually out of fear that their first offer could be far too different from the other sides' first offer and subsequently causes the entire negotiation to fall apart.

What Is Breaking the Ice?

Ice breaking is light conversation that helps both parties build rapport prior to negotiations. You can start by talking about each other's background and interests, or you can also start by praising the other parties' organization. The goal of ice breaking is to change competitive negotiation into cooperative negotiation.

Step 2: The Negotiation Process

The main part of the negotiation process is trying to narrow the gap between the two parties by finding a win-win outcome. In general, if you focus on how to manipulate or persuade the other person, the likelihood of a satisfactory outcome will decrease. Therefore, honest exchange of opinions can be much more successful for a win-win outcome. For example, if the used car customer only has $11,000, you can try to create some financial plan for the customer or if they have more cash, you could charge a higher price but add other options that may be of interest to the customers, such as a warranty or maintenance routine.

Step 3: The Final Step in Negotiations

Some negotiations will not reach an agreement. However, in most cases, it is probably best for each party to concede to each other's demands to reach a mutually beneficial outcome. For example, you could concede $1,000 on the selling price to $12,000 and offer other options, such as a 6-month engine warranty.

Now let us take a look at different types of negotiations. Generally, negotiations can be distributive or integrative. Distributive negotiations are viewed as a "zero-sum game." Whatever is being negotiated is seen as having a fixed value and how this fixed-value "pie" is distributed between the negotiating parties indicates what distributive negotiation is. On the other hand, integrative negotiations move toward an integrated, mutual agreement where both parties work together to maximize the size of the pie. Here, value creation and the seeking of one's own interest occur simultaneously. Not very many negotiations are purely distributive. In most cases both parties in the negotiations can combine their interest, even though their interests and goals may clash initially.

Internationally, Koreans are renowned negotiators, but they

often do not think so of themselves. Koreans are known as stubborn negotiators and they tend to negotiate in a distributive style. What makes negotiating with Koreans even more difficult is that, as aforementioned, they often do not speak explicitly. This forces their negotiating partners to be keenly aware of the situation and understand the context of their conversations. Koreans also tend to be weaker in finding creative win-win solutions.

Conversely, Koreans often view foreign negotiators as highly competent, goal-oriented, and not as concerned with procedural justice or honor. This belief in fact exacerbates Korean's stubbornness in negotiations. Koreans also tend to think that foreign negotiators are more aggressive and diplomatic in tough negotiations. As we have already mentioned several times, they place a high value on "relationships" established before and during the negotiation process. Therefore, Koreans try to find common ground with their negotiating party and develop personal friendships with them by inviting them to dinners or other social functions. They will also try to foster a long-term relationship.

Before going to the negotiation table, Koreans try to be prepared and collect as much data as possible about the other side. They collect all of the data they can because of their holistic approach to tasks. Because Korean culture is very hierarchical and values formality, it is important to follow this tradition throughout the negotiation process. This is especially important during the initial stage when relationships between the negotiating parties have not yet been formed. Generally, larger corporations have superior data collection capabilities on both personal and professional information.

Case Study

Negotiating Styles

Mr. Park has a meeting today with a negotiating team from Norway. The team leader, Mr. Aksel Bergstad, is a big and tall man with a thick beard. His intimidating appearance and loud voice, coupled with his tenacious conversational style and sweeping gestures intimidated the other parties at the negotiating table. Furthermore, his casual dress and addressing others by their first names made Mr. Park and the other Koreans uncomfortable. During their negotiation, Mr. Bergstad also quickly moved on to the next subject before the Koreans had a chance to ask any questions, which startled the Koreans. Why did the Koreans get startled in this situation?

Expert Opinion Maintaining formality in the initial stages of negotiations is very important to Koreans because their culture highly values formality and hierarchy. Thus, they expected to be addressed by their position rather than their first names. Recall our discussion of titles and names in Chapter 4. While titles and positions are not the only important factors for Koreans, proper use of titles and respect for position can be a way of showing respect for Korean culture and lead to a favorable impression.

To Koreans who expected mutual respect and mild mannered conversations based on their culture, Mr. Bergstad's overpowering manner and seemingly-disrespectful conversational style was likely very unexpected and startling. Moreover, to Koreans who are very cautious at first meetings, Mr. Bergstad's casual style may have been offensive. This example shows that it is a good idea to try to understand the other party's culture and tradition throughout the negotiation process especially if they are from another culture.

Summary of Chapter 5

1. Communication

- Communication is an action taken to share information between individuals and departments to make decisions and execute tasks efficiently.

2. Characteristics of Koreans and Korean Groups Concerning Communication

- Koreans tend to keep their distance before they establish personal relationships. However, once someone is accepted as a member of their group, newcomers are quickly assimilated into the spirit of the workplace.
- Once a relationship is forged through shared meals or drinks, they will quickly become very open and affectionate.
- Koreans often identify themselves as members of groups. They have a strong sense of belonging to a group and sometimes they sacrifice their individual interests for the group.

3. Features of Korean Communication

- Koreans often do not say everything they want to express. They rely on different tones of voice, facial expressions, context, and how they start the conversation to fully express their message.
- Top-down communications and directives are sometimes not clearly delivered because of a lack of explicit communication. Thus, it is important for employees to confirm their senior managers' direction clearly.
- Koreans do not like confrontation when conflicts arise and they prefer to resolve their conflicts implicitly.
- The Korean culture of valuing formality is also manifested in intra-organizational communication. Communications within an organization often use appropriate honorific expressions according to age and rank to show respect.

4. Negotiation

- What makes negotiating with Koreans even more difficult is that they often do not speak explicitly. This forces their negotiating partners to be keenly aware of the situation and the context of their conversation.
- Koreans place high value on relationships established before and during the negotiation process. Therefore, they try to find common ground with their negotiating party and develop personal friendships with them by inviting them to dinners or other social functions. They will also try to foster a long-term relationship.
- Korean culture emphasizes harmonious relationships and Koreans are collectivistic, hierarchical, and are used to receiving a superior's instructions. Therefore, they are averse to conflicts and arguments, and especially do not welcome open confrontations.

Chapter 06

Working Relationships with Koreans I

A corporation's business activity is largely dependent on the culture of its home. Therefore, Korea's business activity is largely based on Korean culture and finds its roots in the Eastern culture. In this chapter, we will look into the characteristics of Korean business activities and environments as well as comparing them with those of other countries as well.

In a company with culturally diverse workforce, misunderstandings can be common. However, as we learned in Chapter 2, one cannot judge right or wrong on cultural differences. This requires us to try to understand one another and cooperate to find the best solution for each organization. In this chapter, we will provide fundamental understanding of the way Koreans approach their business activities. Moreover, through case studies, we will learn how to apply these in actual working environment with Koreans.

First of all, let us take a look at what makes a successful manager in Korea and what Koreans think of loyalty, motivation, compensation, sources of authority, feedback and follow-up, performance appraisals, and job mobility. We will cover working relationships in business in Chapter 7.

1

A Successful Manager's Characteristics

In general, organizations formulate strategies to meet its organizational objectives and allocate tasks to its members accordingly. Managers must allocate resources effectively, facilitate smooth teamwork through appropriate guidance and evaluate whether tasks are accomplished accordingly to achieve the goals.

What makes a successful manager? This could be different depending on the culture or the company's situation, but generally, a successful manager has both leadership and management skills. Then what kind of manager would be considered a successful manager in Korea? Traditionally in Korea, academic background and networks were the most important factors in doing business. We learned in Chapter 3 how important education is for Koreans. Even though the caste system no longer exists in Korea, top government and management positions were only attainable for the highly educated, so that education was the only way to raise one's social status. Furthermore, such higher positions offered access to an exclusive network of governmental, financial, and academic elites formed by common academic background or business ties.

This elite network further developed with nepotism, a common Korean characteristic that refers to depending on academic background or regions. Since the Korean government played a leading role during the beginning of Korea's economic growth period, corporations needed to maintain a close relationship with the government in order to obtain various licenses and financial support. Thus, managers that had connections with top government officials were seen as competent managers.

What Is Nepotism?

Koreans try to find common ground to establish a relationship with the people they meet. This is also the case when doing business.
When Koreans meet a stranger, they always tend to want to identify if they belong to any common group with the stranger. By asking about one's hometown, place of residence, previous visits to Korea or even hobbies, Koreans try to find similarities in the smallest things. They like to form relationships by finding a common group between themselves and strangers, and will always ask where they are from and which school they attended. Some of the most important affiliations that Koreans consider are kinship, academic cliques, and regional background. These three factors affect Korean society profoundly.

However, since the economic crisis of the late 1990s, the importance of academic cliques has gradually subsided, and Korean corporations have become increasingly less network-oriented and more task-oriented. Back when lifetime employment and a seniority-based culture were prevalent, people could not quickly react to the fast-changing business environment. Plus, as globalization progressed rapidly, the importance of networks based on academic cliques subsided in Korea. Global networks were created based more on capability than academic cliques, and this became the new business standard. Additionally, less transparent business management practices gradually started to change towards management based on principles of global standards. Consequently, an individual's capability became more important than his or her background.

Generally, Korean corporations prefer generalist managers than specialists. It is believed that a manager should be well rounded and not skewed toward a specific field. Since managing employees is emphasized at the executive level, corporations prefer generalists while specialists with knowledge of specific fields are preferred for middle managers.

Korean companies are generally managed according to a job rotation scheme. The number of specialists per organization is low unless it is an exception like a research division. This is because people tend to think that it is harder for specialists, like engineers, to advance to executive management in hierarchical organizations. Therefore more prefer to become generalists who are more likely to be promoted rather than specialists. Nowadays, there is a trend toward higher job satisfaction and ample financial reward as a specialist. This is partly due to the rise of individualism that limits interest in others while focusing on increasing one's own benefits and happiness.

The Job Rotation Scheme

The job rotation scheme is a human resource management policy adopted for efficient staff relocation by rotating supervisors of sales, planning, management and other departments every two to three years. It is a policy that develops generalists with experiences in all functions rather than experts in specific functions. This system allows for employees to experience a variety of roles and acquire knowledge and many Korean corporations implement it as a part of career development.

Where does the power of Korean managers come from? Korean managers' sources of power are their position, seniority in the hierarchy-based society, and their experience. Work experience in the rapidly growing Korean economy is especially a valuable asset that enabled Korean managers to absorb new things quickly. However, global businesses as well as Korean firms highly value creativity today, increasing the importance of experience as well as creativity.

An individual's ability, networks, and previous work experience are also helpful sources of power to business managers. Other management power comes from the evaluation and the compensation of his or her staff. Most members of staff want their managers to be fair, have good communication skills and help build a foundation for their career development. On the other hand, managers want their staff to perform well, cooperate with the rest of the team members and hope they are loyal to them and the organization.

To Koreans, not only is the company they work for important, but also what kind of a superior they work for is also very important. This is because many individuals spend a lot of time at work, the turnover rate is low and many relationships with their bosses turn into personal ones.

In a recent survey conducted by a Korean job portal site, 76.8 percent responded that they have considered quitting or changing their jobs due to conflict with their immediate supervisor.[1] This implies that when working with a great manager, workers will have strong loyalty and do their best, resulting in higher quality work.

Let us briefly look at the managerial style that is approved in a hierarchical organization. Korean organizations are hierarchical; a hierarchical organization is an organization that is a relationship-based rather than work-based. Therefore, considerate managers are sometimes evaluated as more competent and capable in hierarchical organizations than those who evaluate fairly.

Case Study

A Successful Manager

A new foreign manager has been assigned to your team. However, you have little clue as to who is coming. You are guessing that it would either be Mr. Kim or Mr. Lee. Mr. Kim is a manager known to have great capabilities and is a person who judges his staff fairly and objectively. On the other hand, Mr. Lee is not even close to Mr. Kim when it comes to his capabilities or fairness, but is known for his warm consideration for his staff. He allows his staff to handle personal affairs during work hours when there are family issues and when his staff finds themselves in trouble, he tries to help out personally. Which of the two managers would you like to be in charge of your department?

Expert Opinion Of these two completely different managers, who would be better and more efficient? Whose leadership would be considered more desirable in Korea? In most situations, Mr. Kim would be more efficient but in case of an emergency situation that requires immediate overtime, Mr. Lee will be a much more effective leader. In a vertically structured organization with strong relational bonds, people do not mind working on tasks outside of their job descriptions. Therefore most Koreans would evaluate the more considerate Mr. Lee to be a better manager. However, the standard of a successful manager could be different in the West due to the cultural differences.

Westerners who tend to be more individualistic might consider a manager who has great capabilities and fair judgment to be better than the one who considers relationships more important. In Western culture, workplace or colleagues are not viewed as equivalent to family, thus it is generally understood that people should resolve personal issues by themselves. In a similar vein, they may feel uncomfortable with a boss being considerate about their personal problems. As such, we can see that a successful manager can vary depending on the culture.

2
Loyalty

During the 1960s to 1980s when Korea lacked quality jobs, employee loyalty towards companies was very strong. Also during this period, Koreans were brought up in extended families so they naturally had acquired a strong sense of loyalty. Likewise, companies took good care of their employees and treated them as family.

This all changed in the late 1990s after the economic crisis, as the idea of a lifetime job was shattered and changed the concept of workplace loyalty in Korea. However, the older generation still considers loyalty very important and sometimes puts the company before themselves. Some employees who decide to move on to new jobs remain in their positions until the company finds a successor, even if that means staying beyond their contract. This is because Koreans do not like to create hard feelings when they leave. As we learned in Chapter 1, this is also rooted in the Korean concept of pursuing purity. In Korea, changing one's job frequently for one's benefit is thought to taint their purity.

Application of purity to loyalty can be found in the West as well. For example, Carl Ripken, Jr. played his entire Major League Baseball career with the Baltimore Orioles. Also known as the "Iron Man," he is best known for having set the record for playing the most consecutive games (total 2,632 games) in the Major League. Born in Maryland, Ripken had strong roots in the Baltimore area and his father was the coach for the Orioles. Throughout his successful career, despite having received offers from other Major League teams, he stayed with the Orioles until he retired in 2001. He remains one of the most beloved and respected players of all time.

The concept of loyalty is becoming increasingly diluted to new generations joining the workforce. The new generation of Koreans does not hesitate to change jobs and interprets loyalty toward the company as doing their best at work. Another type of loyalty can be towards a boss who has great leadership skills. In such cases, his staff will do almost anything for the boss and show strong support in front of others. This is because in Korean organizational culture, work relationships often grow into family-like personal relationships. Hence, when a boss moves to another company, his or her staff follow suit at times.

In Korean organizations, *hoesik* is often used to increase loyalty to the company. Along the same line, there are also company picnic days, field day, volunteer days and other group activities. Many Korean companies regularly hold field days or hiking days by smaller teams or as company-wide activities. Korean companies usually hold these events during the weekend to avoid affecting working hours.

The younger generation of today does not accept unreasonable situations. They do not willingly attend company events that they are not interested in. Korean companies are aware of such change that they try to inspire loyalty by forming interest groups among employees rather than holding mandatory events on a company-wide scale. Thus, it is necessary for the Korean companies to actively support most of the interest-group activities within the company.

3

Motivation

Let us learn about what kind of motivation is used efficiently and effectively in Korea and what kinds of motivation are preferred in other countries.

Motivation derives from the Latin word "movere," meaning "make it move." It is defined as a psychological process that continuously brings out the voluntary action that focuses on the motivated goal from the group action. Academically, it is defined as stimulating a certain person to take action toward achieving a goal, enabling the person to have a motive, inducing a specific action, and having the person continue it. Essentially, stimulation and motive should be provided to achieve a goal. Someone is highly motivated if they do not give up.

Motivation is divided into monetary motivation such as bonuses, incentives, stock dividends, etc., and non-monetary motivation such as promotions, self-development opportunities, recognition, empowerment, and flexible working schedule. Of these, an organization chooses motivation methods that best fit its culture, individual's tendencies, and situation. Recently in Korea, motivation based on self-development has become common. Such motivation through training can increase loyalty toward the company as well as reduce turnover rate.

Motivation can differ depending on cultural differences. This can be explained by Maslow's hierarchy of needs. For example, people in risk and uncertainty-averse countries like Korea or Japan can be more motivated to satisfy security needs than self-actualization needs, in comparison to Americans who tend to be more adventurous.

In Korea, civil service has been considered to be the "job of the gods" and has always been ranked high in employment preferences. This is because civil servants rarely face risk of termination compared to regular companies. It illustrates that Koreans find stable employment to be more attractive than a challenging one.

In Northern European countries such as Sweden, Denmark and Norway, which have great welfare systems, people emphasize quality of life rather than exceeding productivity norms or a goal. Therefore, they tend to be more motivated through things such as sense of belonging, relationships, and social fellowship. We should be aware of the fact that the rank and magnitude of needs are different, depending on cultures.

Now, let us think about D. McClelland's Achievement Motivation Theory. McClelland explained that human beings are motivated by the need for achievement, affiliation, and power. He first emphasized the need for achievement and after studying Indian entrepreneurs, found that the need for achievement motivates humans regardless of culture. However, people from non-Anglo American countries, such as Chile, India or Portugal, have little need for achievement and therefore the need for achievement itself cannot be an efficient motivator.

Moreover, psychologist F. Herzberg emphasized that in extremely individualistic, productivity-focused and masculine cultures, job enrichment can be a motivation tool. In Northern Europe, where welfare standards are high, quality of the relationships at workplace can be a better motivator than job enrichment.

Now, let us look into the motivational methods of Korean companies. Korean companies generally use two methods to motivate their employees. One is to manage career development and the other is to boost morale. Motivation through managing career development includes expanding responsibility, providing more opportunities in work experience and relevant training. Empowerment and a shared vision are effective for this type of motivation. Traditional managers who scold subordinates and embarrass them in front of others to motivate performance are becoming increasingly unpopular. The alternative method, boosting morale, includes complimenting and encouraging. Considering that Koreans prefer emotional conversation, complimenting is the most common motivational method.

Also, as in other countries, monetary compensation is one of the core motivators for Koreans as well. Promotion and recognition or career development opportunities are also major motivational strategies. Another motivational strategy is to appeal to the Koreans' keen need for sense of belonging, with the pride of "working at a reputable company" and "job stability."

Case Study

Motivation 1

Jana works at the Czech branch of a Korean company. Today, she looks very disappointed coming out of her Korean boss's office. Jana recently wrote a proposal for a very important client that was very well received and signed. Her boss was very satisfied and as compensation for Jana, he decided to send her abroad to the biggest annual conference in the industry. This year's conference was held in Seoul, so Jana's boss thought it would be great compensation for Jana since she works for a Korean company. Her boss had already made up his mind and had paid for all of the conference-related expenses for Jana. However, that was the problem. Jana had already notified that she could not attend overseas conferences because of her children. So Jana was unfortunately given the compensation of an overseas conference that she could not attend. How would you have felt if you were Jana? What was the problem and how should the problem be solved?

Expert Opinion Jana will understand that her Korean boss made a thoughtful decision. However, the problem arose from Jana's oversight on her current situation. Jana already notified her company that she could not leave her kids to go to the conference but her boss understood this with a Korean mindset. In Korea, if one cannot take care of children due to company business, other family members will often take care of the children while the parents are away. This is because Koreans tend to take work more seriously than household situations. Unfortunately the Korean boss figured it would be the same in the Czech Republic.

Jana's Korean boss thought that attending the conference would be beneficial for Jana in developing her career and that the sense of recognition would be a great motivation for her as well. As mentioned, this is a typical motivation tool in Korean companies so Jana's Korean boss must have found it natural to use it. In this situation, it seems that the Korean boss is the source of the problem rather than Jana. While his intentions to compensate his subordinate were good, he failed to consider Jana's personal situation first and did not consider the cultural difference in motivating the employees.

When their boss compliments on their performance and offers compensation, Korean employees generally reply modestly by saying, "I'm fine." However, this usually is not a way of turning down an offer, so misunderstandings can happen. If Jana misses the compensation opportunity by not being able to go on a trip, the trip would not have been a motivation and may actually decrease her drive to work. Therefore, if Jana cannot accept the intended offer as a motivator, the manager should understand her situation and offer a different compensation.

Motivation 2

Jana planned a new products launch show in Prague and invited buyers from England, Vietnam and India. The launch show was a huge success and there were over five new contracts signed as a result of the show. Many more are currently under negotiation with positive prospects. The company was largely depending on the success of these products for survival and Jana's performance was truly significant in this regard. The company is debating whether they should give her a 600 percent increase in her salary for the month or a one-level promotion on her marketing team. How would you like to be motivated if you were Jana?

Expert Opinion The company wants to provide Jana with a positive motivation for her great performance and the company is debating whether to provide motivation through monetary compensation or promotion. What kind of motivator will Jana want? If she were a typical Korean employee, she would want promotion as a motivator. Here, monetary compensation might provide instant motivation but promotion would be a very significant motivator in Korean society, where hierarchy and reputation mean a lot. Monetary compensation can offer an instant, one-time motivation, but a promotion will have more long-term effects and can help when seeking new jobs.

4

Compensation

Wages are the profits that a worker receives in return for the labor that is provided to the company. Compensation is all other benefits a worker receives from the company besides wages, in monetary and non-monetary form. Compensation is divided into economic rewards and non-economic rewards. Monetary rewards include wages and bonuses, while non-economic rewards include non-economic elements such as satisfaction, sense of achievement, promotions, and employee benefit packages. Compensation is a human resource management tool and can be utilized to accelerate achievement of strategic goals.

When constructing a compensation system, a variety of compensation types other than monetary rewards can be used, such as encouragement and performance recognition. To achieve this, many advanced companies use recognition and celebration program. This is a policy of giving awards to people who have performed with distinction in a specific field. Though practices differ from company to company, employees generally receive a thank you letter from the CEO as well as recognition and celebration from their peers by being featured in company newsletters.

Now, let us work on the following scenario before we look into the Korean compensation system.

Case Study

Compensation for Team Performance

This happened at a Seoul office training team of a Korean company. The training team developed a new learning management system for the employees. The idea for this system originally came from director Lee, who outlined all of the plans and schedules for this system and led this project. After six months of hard work with his teammates, the new learning management system was established with very positive assessments throughout top management and the employees. The company was very satisfied with the team's success and especially wanted to reward director Lee with monetary compensation for his exceptional performance. When the company offered a 200 percent increase in his pay for one month, director Lee felt uncomfortable being the only recipient of a bonus since the whole team had worked on the project together. In the end, the company replaced the compensation offered to director Lee with a *hoesik* for the whole team. Why do you think director Lee refused individual compensation? What do you make of this situation?

Expert Opinion When it comes to receiving compensation, Koreans have a subgroup culture where they consider themselves as equals within the subgroup. Koreans consider recognition of the team as the highest importance and then focus on their own recognition within the team. If the team's performance was great but one individual's contribution was exceptional and the company only wants to give financial compensation to that person, that person would find the situation rather uncomfortable. This could potentially destroy the team's cooperation. The rewarded person may want to share the financial compensation equally with the rest of the team.

Here, director Lee thinks that since it was a team project the compensation should be for the entire team, even though he single-handedly led the team with great responsibility. If he were the only person financially compensated, he would feel sorry for the rest of the team and the team members would feel disappointed, thinking that their effort was nothing compared to his. In fact, if director Lee alone were to receive the compensation, he could have problems as a leader in the future. If the company still gave him the bonus in spite of his refusal, he would probably want to share the bonus with the team by having a *hoesik* with the team or in other ways.

That is why in circumstances like this, Korean companies prefer to compensate by giving bonus points for new opportunities or promotions, rather than giving financial bonuses to an individual with exceptional performance.

Many Korean companies still have a hierarchy-based wage system, but many international companies use performance-based systems. Special compensation varies in accordance with each company's policies but is usually in the form of material rewards such as bonuses, gift cards, and stock options. Different types of compensation include: paid leave, overseas trips, restaurant gift certificates, and training opportunities. In Korea, teams are congratulated for their performances primarily by having *hoesik*. Moreover, recognition programs such as the "employee of the month" system are often used.

5

Sources of Authority

What are the sources of authority in organizations in your culture? Let us learn about the various sources of authority.

Authority requires a premise that there is a social relation of more than two people or a group. In addition, authority includes not only the real ability but potential ability that exists in social relations. Authority is the ability to induce or change an individual or a group regardless of their opinions. It means that an individual or a group has dominance over another individual or another group.

Jurisdiction is an official power that one individual possesses due to the position that he or she has in an organization. For example, in organizations, superiors have a legitimate power over subordinates. That is, jurisdiction is an element of authority and it emphasizes legitimacy. Jurisdiction also means a right to dominate an individual or a group. Jurisdiction is generally considered a downward flow and superiors' jurisdiction takes effect when subordinates acknowledge and accept it.

Influence is the total amount of power that an individual or a group can exert to change another person or group's manner, mindset, attitude, actions, etc. Therefore, influence is sometimes used as a synonym of authority. However, influence is the superordinate concept to authority and authority is the superordinate concept to jurisdiction. That is, influence is a bigger concept than authority and authority is a bigger concept than jurisdiction.

Definition of Jurisdiction, Authority and Influence

Concept	Definition
Jurisdiction	An official power that an individual possesses due to the position that he or she has in an organization
Authority	An individual or a group procuring dominance over another individual or a group
Influence	The total amount of power that an individual or a group can exert to change another person or group's manner, mindset, attitude, actions, etc.

The authority of Korean managers comes from their position, hierarchy, and experience. Good educational background and work experience at reputable firms also help in maintaining authority. From another point of view, a manager's authority could come from his/her power to evaluate the staff's performance and respective compensation. Moreover, another important element is how much a manager is recognized by his supervisors. If the manager has good networks with outsiders and can provide key solutions to problems arising outside the organization, the manager will have more power.

6

Feedback & Follow-up

The feedback and follow-up process is the business activity that best showcases the Korean roots in relationship-focused culture. As we saw in Chapter 5, Koreans believe that feedback to each other include personal feelings. This is why negative feedback is always delivered in indirect and circumvent ways. Now, we will look into how feedback and follow-up processes are handled in Korean companies.

First, let us define feedback and see what makes a good feedback. In corporations, feedback is an essential part of the information given to individuals in a working environment that tells them how they are performing based on various goals. Positive and constructive feedbacks are essential elements in the monitoring process. Ineffective feedback may create results far worse than giving no feedback at all.

What is positive and constructive feedback? First of all, feedback should be specific. It should focus on specific actions of subordinates. For example, let us assume that you gave your subordinate a simple, "excellent job" as feedback. In this case, "excellent job" does not specify which action the feedback was intended for, which in turn confuses the subordinate in his/her future actions. Second, feedback should be timely. Immediate feedback is necessary in order to prevent subpar performance from becoming the norm. Especially, constructive or negative feedback should not be delayed.

Third, feedback should be balanced. Positive and constructive feedback produce different results, but both types of feedback are necessary and valuable methods. Positive feedback motivates employees and creates pride while constructive feedback positively affects performance. Therefore, using a strategy that balances these two types of feedback is optimal.

Historically in Korean companies, no feedback from the top was understood as having no problems or issues on the completed task and was regarded as good news. However, these days, the younger generation wants more feedback to help advance their careers. The most favored method of feedback in Korea is the private feedback. That is, Koreans do not like receiving feedback publicly. In a Korean company, feedback may be given casually in everyday work as well as in informal settings such as over meals or tea. In fact, many companies provide only informal feedback and do not provide official feedback. This is because the relationship between superiors and subordinates is often public and personal in Korea.

The feedback process varies widely by organizations and is dependent on the style of management that is used. In a hierarchical organization, a manager's positive feedback can significantly motivate the employees. However, negative feedback in a public setting should be avoided since it may embarrass the recipient. The best way to give feedback is to do it one-on-one in informal settings and focus on the areas for improvement rather than mistakes. Direct criticism could hurt the recipient's feelings and may be interpreted as a personal resentment. It should be noted that in male-dominant companies, managers may use an individual's mistake as an opportunity to set an example for the rest of the group. For example, if an employee is often late to work, the manager wouldn't give feedback directly to the employee but would caution all of the employees about tardiness in a meeting.

In terms of feedback, Korean managers think that they have the responsibility to finish their projects and follow-up on their subordinates' projects as well. Guiding the staff to successfully finish projects is an essential requirement for managers. However, excessive involvement and micro-managing will result in staff's dissatisfaction.

Case Study

A Way to Give Feedback

You are the leader of the global team at the British office. You noticed that one employee does not participate much in meetings. She is a Korean employee named Joohee, and although she seems to know a lot and answers all of questions correctly, she never asks questions or provides ideas. Her performance and the way she talks show that she is very professional and is very capable. Although she has great potential, seeing her not participate in the meetings made you question whether she is engaged with the team or even interested in the team at all. How would you resolve this situation as a team leader?

Expert Opinion Let us recall the characteristics of Koreans we've already learned. As we learned in Chapters 1 and 3, discussion can be animated amongst people of the same hierarchy in Korean culture, but discussion with a supervisor is difficult because of the hierarchical culture. In fact, Koreans prefer to listen to what the supervisor has to say. If there is anything that one wants to say to the supervisor, such discussions take place before the meeting. Of course, the problem may be because of Joohee's personality, but she also may be having difficulties with the language barrier. When a meeting is led in English, those not fluent in English are often cannot be very assertive about their opinions and end up listening most of the time.

If I were the leader of this team, I would first have a private, informal meeting with Joohee. I would start by complimenting her on her ability and carefully ask why she does not participate more in team meetings. If it is because of her culture, I would recommend that she share her ideas at the team meetings and participate more. I would also explain that this will improve her performance and will be a valuable contribution to the company overall. As a team leader, you have a responsibility to maximize your team's performance, so when you find that Joohee is not actively participating in team meetings, you need to find out why she isn't doing so and give her appropriate feedback to encourage contribution. However, considering Korean culture, this feedback will be more effective if it is delivered in a private meeting along with compliments.

7

Performance Appraisals

Reasonable and fair performance assessment and respective compensation can effectively motivate the employees to work harder. The purpose of the performance appraisal system is to focus on the core strengths of the employees in order to maximize achievement of the organization's business goals. Moreover, it is to motivate the development of an individual's abilities as well as to foster a performance-based culture in the company. Also, a performance appraisal system that is based on objective judgment and linked to fair compensation ultimately enhances employee satisfaction and efficiency. This in turn, contributes to achieving the company's goals.

Now, let us learn about Korea's performance appraisal system.

Koreans do not find performance appraisals pleasant, but take them very seriously. They understand performance appraisal as part of a system they must endure to assess their performance. Most companies appraise performance once or twice a year and a few companies appraise it continuously. Most companies use various evaluation tools depending on the company's situation and goals. Recently, some companies have been using 360-degree feedback with self-evaluation. 360-degree feedback is a tool that provides each employee the opportunity to receive performance feedback from his or her supervisor and four to eight peers, reporting staff members, coworkers, and customers. The individual then responds to the 360-degree feedback through a self-assessment. In the evaluation process, the most important factor is likely the opinion of the employee's supervisor.

When assessing performance in an organizational setting, job outcome and job behavior should both be considered. For example, for an employee of an appliance store, the total amount of sales or unit sales would be the job outcome and the method of approaching the customers in order to sell the appliances would be the job behavior. If the sales-team manager of the appliance store only focuses on job outcomes in the performance appraisal of its employees, the sales staff will focus only on their short-term goals, sales, and not on customer service, which would lead to a bad impression with the customers. Also, it could escalate competition among employees. On the other hand, if they are only assessed on job behavior, it may motivate them to provide good customer service but wouldn't necessarily increase sales. Therefore, all performance appraisal systems should include job outcome and job behavior. However, this general assessment may be rather subjective, so it works best when there is trust and cooperation within an organization.

Koreans tend to approach evaluations in a macroscopic and general way. Performance appraisal systems assess performance based on the goal set at the beginning of the year. However, Koreans emphasize the process of achieving the goal and job behavior. Koreans also value diligence and sincerity. Let us recall Chapter 2 where we learned the differences between Eastern and Western cultures. Asians tend to conceptualize objects as a whole from a broad perspective rather than looking at an individual part. In similar a vein, Koreans take a broad view in their approach to performance appraisal. They not only assess performance based on personal goals but also on diligence and relationships with coworkers. This performance appraisal system comes from the tendency to look at the whole picture.

Also, Korean organizations usually do not just assess results when a project goes awry. They take into account the process of arriving at the final result. If the team or the individuals tried their best but could not achieve their goal due to external factors, then job outcome is not the only factor that is considered and in most cases, no direct penalty is inflicted. In such situations, they consider the effort that was put into achieving this goal throughout the entire process. However, if there were many problems during the process, they will make sure they deal with these issues before they move on, regardless of the outcome. Ultimately, this indicates that Korean organizations expect their staff to make an effort to achieve their goals as well as during the process.

Diligence is another important variable that cannot be overlooked in performance appraisal. At times, diligence can make up for sub-par performance. Relationships with others also play a major role in performance appraisal. It is important not to make enemies in the organization and an individual's personality, potential and attitude are considered very important in the performance appraisal system for this reason.

Case Study

Assessment

Peter is a very capable employee in a Korean company's UK office. All of his projects are completed to a high standard and in time for the deadline. However, when he feels that he is right, he is completely inflexible in his opinions. This always creates problems for the rest of the team but when it comes to results, he has a very positive attitude and outstanding ability. Now the performance appraisal period is just around the corner. If you were his supervisor, what would you consider when assessing his performance?

Expert Opinion In any country, performance appraisal systems should be fair. As we mentioned before, job outcomes and job behavior should both be included in performance appraisal systems. If only job outcome is assessed, Peter is outstanding and should receive an excellent evaluation but there is clearly room for improvement in maintaining good relationship with his team. Good teamwork is quite valuable and efforts to get along with team members are just as important as individual ability. Moreover, good teamwork plays a critical role in an organization's work efficiency. Therefore, when evaluated on both factors, Peter would not be the assessed well. In order to improve, Peter needs more self awareness about his impact on others and needs to work on developing a more inclusive and flexible approach with his team.

In Korean organizations, seniority culture still exists, which often leads to unfair performance appraisal. For example, let us say that Mr. Lee, Mr. Kim, and Mr. Park all work in the same department and all three have an opportunity to be promoted to a director position this year. Among the three candidates, Mr. Lee is the oldest and has satisfactory performance so his team will elect him as their favored candidate in the race for promotion. The team will then give Mr. Lee a favorable performance assessment in order to increase his chances for promotion over the other departments' candidates competing for the same position. Here, two mechanisms are at work: first, the seniority culture leads the team to decide that Mr. Lee should be promoted over the other two younger competent managers. Second, the sub-group mentality of the Koreans leads the team to manipulate the performance appraisal so that their team's candidate, Mr. Lee, would be more likely to be promoted for the position before other teams. In this case, the team becomes the sub-group that the team members strongly identify with.

Ultimately, this means that sometimes those with excellent performance may receive an inferior assessment in the appraisal process. While Koreans certainly do not enjoy this, most try to understand by reasoning that they may benefit from this same practice one day. This may appear as a bizarre performance appraisal system for Westerners who value fair appraisals. This is the case of the Korean sub-group mentality in the works (in this case, the team is the sub-group).

8

Job Mobility

In the past, Korean companies used to offer "lifetime employment," but ever since the 1997 economic crisis, companies began to let go of employees with sub-par performance. At the same time, employee loyalty toward their companies began to wane. Nowadays, many Koreans are experiencing more job mobility than in the past and employees in international companies tend to change jobs more often than those who work in Korean companies.

Koreans traditionally believe that those who frequently change jobs lack loyalty toward the company. Recall our previous discussion on purity and traditionalism. Koreans fear that such people will change jobs again when they have the slightest dissatisfaction and those with a history of job mobility are sometimes less likely to be hired.

In other countries, changing jobs is considered a healthy way to develop one's career or increase one's salary. However, in Korea, such people are considered to have problems getting along with others or lack important skills and characteristics needed to be successful in business. Therefore, interviewers will often want to know the reason for relocation if the potential hire has a history of changing jobs. Of course, some Korean employees change jobs to develop their careers or to increase their salaries, but human resource directors do not view this favorably either. In Korea, it is considered sensible to work at a company for at least five years.

Summary of chapter 6

1. A Successful Manager's Characteristics

- As globalization rapidly progressed, the importance of academic cliques based on an elite network subsided in Korea. A global network was created based on working ability instead of academic cliques and became the standard of global business.

2. Loyalty

- From the 1960s to 1980s when Korea lacked quality jobs, employee loyalty toward companies was very strong. Also, during this period, Koreans were brought up in extended families so they naturally had acquired a strong sense of loyalty.
- In the late 1990s after the economic crisis, the idea of a lifetime job was shattered and changed the concept of workplace loyalty in Korea. The older generation still considers loyalty very important and sometimes puts the company before themselves.

3. Motivation

- Korean companies generally use two methods to motivate their employees. One is to manage career development and the other is to boost morale. Alternatively, they may use complimenting and encouraging. Similar to other countries, financial compensation is a key motivator for Koreans. Promotion, recognition, and opportunities for career development are also important motivators.

4. Compensation

- Koreans display subgroup tendencies when it comes to receiving compensation. They also consider themselves equal within that respective subgroup. Koreans consider the recognition of their team as most important. They acknowledge their own achievements after the group has been recognized.

5. Sources of Authority

- The authority of Korean managers comes from their position, hierarchy, and experience. A good educational background and work experience at reputable firms also help in maintaining authority. Another important element is how much a manager is recognized by his supervisors. If the manager has good networks with outsiders and can provide key solutions to problems arising outside the organization, the manager will have more power.

6. Feedback & Follow-up

- Negative feedback in a public setting should be avoided since it may embarrass the recipient. The best way to give feedback is to do it privately in informal settings and focus on the areas of improvement rather than mistakes. Direct criticism could hurt the recipient's feelings and may be interpreted as a personal resentment.

7. Performance Appraisals

- Koreans tend to approach performance appraisal macroscopically and generally.
- Koreans consider job behavior and the process of reaching the goal very important. Attitude and diligence are highly valued in performance appraisal as well.

8. Job Mobility

- Many Koreans nowadays are experiencing increased job mobility. In addition, employees in international companies tend to change jobs more often than those who work in Korean companies.

Chapter 07

Working Relationships with Koreans II

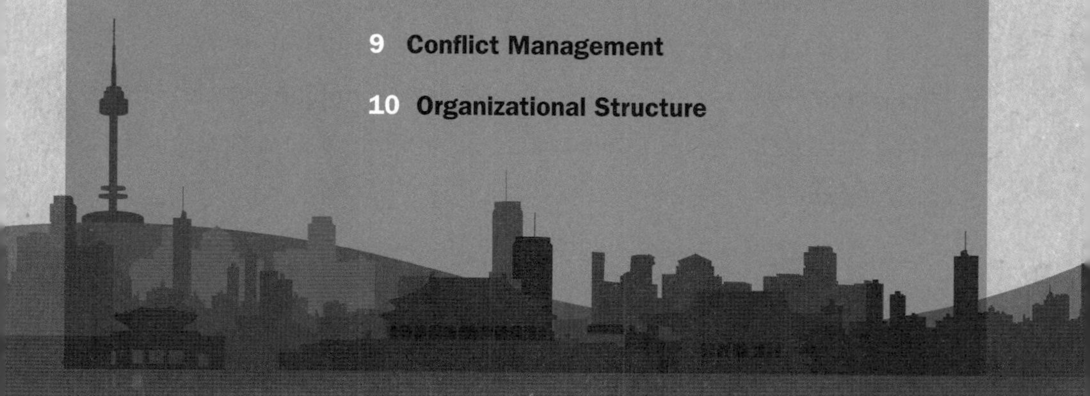

In this chapter, we will learn about working relationships from a task management point of view. We will cover various working relationships in hiring, decision-making, delegation, information sharing, planning, conflict management, teamwork, timelines, and organizational structure to help your comprehensive understanding of the working relationships in Korea.

1
Employment

Today's corporations are experiencing massive changes in their business environments due to factors such as globalization, rapidly developing technology, and a shift toward customer satisfaction. Thus, corporate survival and growth is directly linked with the ability to take proactive measures to adapt to the ever-changing environment. Securing talent is critical in such measures; therefore, strategic recruitment must be developed to procure top-talent. There has been a wave of change in recruitment and interview processes as a result of change in the corporate environment. This is largely related to the shift in the human resource management paradigm of Korean corporations and began around the economic crisis of 1997. Today's corporations are working towards developing unique recruitment plans that utilize various new channels to recruit talent best suited for their needs.

One of the most notable changes in recruitment trends is the high regard for foreign language proficiency. Korea's high foreign dependency in economic development requires foreign language proficiency, which in turn led to the perception that those proficient in foreign languages are also competent at their work. Moreover, as the corporate environment becomes increasingly globalized, corporate needs for foreign language speakers are expanding from just English to various other languages including Spanish, French, Arabic, and Chinese. However, Koreans are far more comfortable learning Chinese or Japanese than learning Latin-based, Western languages because they are linguistically much more similar. So it is often more difficult to recruit fluent speakers of Western languages than of Asian languages.

Also, Korean corporations' preference for creative and challenging talent has been increasing and they spend a lot of time in interviews to recruit such talent. Job aptitude and personality tests have been emphasized more as a result, diversifying and specifying the recruitment process. International talent recruitment has also increased with the growth of multinational corporations.

For entry-level recruitment, the process usually involves resume screening and interviews from open recruitment to find candidates that best fit the organization's needs. A typical recruitment process for experienced applicants usually begins by contacting recruitment agencies. In addition to recruitment agencies, hiring for low-experience positions are sometimes held in open recruitment. When using recruitment agencies, candidates are first screened by the agencies and then screened by the human resources and relevant departments for further interviews. Additional interviews follow depending on positions and recruitment is finalized with managerial approval.

Here is an interesting fact about Korea. All of the major Korean corporations used to hold interviews for each year's new college graduates on the same date. Since working for a major corporation represented prestige, the government mandated a single interview day in order to give as many people a chance as possible. This practice meant that an individual could only receive a job offer from one major corporation. This ties back to the Korea's idea of equality, which was covered in Chapter 1.

Today's younger generation tend to apply for high-paying jobs at reputable companies with short hours. They also prefer the service industry over manufacturing. According to Incruit, a Korean recruiting website, for all publicly traded corporations that recruited in 2010, a total of 1,221,715 candidates applied for 17,195 positions, with the competition at average of 71:1.

The construction industry was the most competitive with the competition ratio of 178:1, followed by the information-communication industry at 121:1 and the automobile industry at 101:1. With respect to size, the competition ratio was 90:1 for large companies, which was higher than the mid-sized enterprises' ratio of 80:1 and the small enterprises' ratio of 33:1. This reflects the hierarchical element of Korean culture where even corporations are ranked in hierarchy. Employment at larger companies is preferred for the younger generation because it saves face and is considered favorable in seeking marriage.

2
Decision-Making

Decision-making is the process of identifying problems and searching, evaluating and selecting appropriate alternatives as the solution. In an organization, not only managers but also employees continuously make decisions. And these decisions affect the decision maker, other relevant people, and ultimately affect the overall performance of the organization.

What are the factors that influence the evaluation of decision outcomes? First is the quality of the decision made. Quality decision-making is selecting the best available alternative among all possible alternatives. The second is the timing of the decision-making. No matter how good it is, untimely decisions are useless. The third factor is how well the decision is received by others. For most organizations, the decision-making process includes not only the decision maker but others as well. Acceptance by others is a good indicator of the quality of the decision made.

Decision-making skills are one of the most important requirements for managers. Top-level managers must be able to make timely decisions based on their analytical skills and experience. In Korea's hierarchical culture, decision-making is usually characterized by a top-down approach. As reflective of the hierarchical culture in Korea, Korean employees tend to favor managers who have good decision-making skills rather than those who suggest.

Decision-making in organizations is mainly done by upper-level managers and the executive management makes most critical decisions. Delegating decisions to lower level managers have become common and the younger generation is motivated by this and accept that the ensuing responsibilities. However, such decision-making processes may differ by culture and require different approaches by stage.

A Step-by-Step Approach to Decision-Making

Decision-making steps include:

1. Problem recognition
2. Search for information
3. Search for alternatives.
4. Alternatives selection
5. Implementation and evaluation

For example, in the problem recognition step, Americans would view this as an opportunity for change and improvement but those from Southeast Asia would more likely accept the status quo rather than to make changes to adapt. Cultural differences would be especially critical in selecting an alternative because of differences in risk management and authoritarian tendencies. Cultures that value challenge will most likely select the high-risk, high-reward alternative while authoritarian cultures will most likely select a decision favored by the authority.

When participating in the decision-making process, Koreans mostly echo their leader's opinion. In Korean society, where people are always aware of others' opinions and want to save face, it is difficult to voice dissent with one's superior or peers. Moreover, they like to refer to precedents and benchmarks from other organizations to help make decisions. This is rooted in the Koreans' tendency to dislike uncertainty, which was discussed in Chapter 5. Koreans try to minimize uncertainty and generally are risk-averse.

Case Study

Decision-Making

Jana recently joined a Korean company's development team where she is the only non-Korean employee. In the final stage of development, a problem arose with the design of the new product. It was discovered that if the company made the product as is, profit would be significantly reduced but with slight modification in design, profits could increase by more than 50 percent than originally expected. A meeting was called to make decision in this situation. The Korean manager suggested that since changing the design at this stage could disrupt the product-launch schedule, they should keep the original design. However, Jana found it strange that no one voiced their opinions and just nodded along with the manager. Jana thought changing the design slightly to significantly increase profitability was the logical choice but found it hard to say so in that environment. Jana wondered if the rest of the team really agreed with the Korean manager and thought it was very strange that nobody disagreed with him. How can we explain this situation to Jana?

Expert Opinion In a hierarchical society like Korea, decisions made by leaders are very important and are accepted accordingly. Raising objections to the leader's opinion at meetings are thought to be offensive and could cause conflict for Koreans, so employees are usually reluctant to disagree.

Then, how should Jana proceed, unfamiliar as she is with this aspect of Korean culture? There are many ways Jana could react but one is to gently share her opinion with the manager in an informal setting. We cannot guarantee that this will change the decision already made by the leader, but she may be able to plan ahead for when the reduced profitably becomes problematic.

In fact, a better solution would be to let the manager know her opinion prior to the decision-making meeting. Another reason the Korean staff may not have actively discussed their opinions during the meeting is because they most likely would have had an informal discussion with the manager prior to the meeting. This is very common in Korea. Also, if the manager's decision is delivered top-down, then the decision will most likely not change.

3
Delegation

Effective delegation is one of the most important prerequisites for a great leader. Delegation refers to when managers empower their subordinates with the necessary power and responsibility to complete a task and ensure that they fully understand how to proceed with the task. Effective delegation ultimately creates motivation for achievement and develops productivity. When managers learn how to rely on subordinates, they themselves also become more motivated and can concentrate more on important strategic issues. However, authority and responsibility of delegation can be very difficult for a new manager. This is especially so when on a tight schedule to launch a new organization or while concentrating on a new, major product or service. So, many managers find it more convenient to continue making decisions themselves as they have in the past. They believe they are at their best when they make their own decisions and do not want to lose their power and authority.

Traditionally, Korean companies have had difficulty with delegation, resulting in a military-like organization. This organizational form proved to be problematic, so today's corporations are strongly encouraging delegation. Managers want to share detailed tasks with their subordinates and delegation is often used as a means of empowerment and motivation. The hierarchical culture in Korea is gradually fading away. On the other hand, some fear that delegation can weaken their position and therefore only delegate nominally or only share partial information when they delegate.

Delegation can range from data collection to technical solutions. Large Korean corporations have specified tasks that are delegated throughout the hierarchy. In such situations, delegated employees often perform their task without understanding the big picture of the overall task. Multinational companies are more likely to delegate tasks by function and job description where managers delegate work according to the employee's competence and the expected outcome.

Because of different communication styles, foreigners may not clearly understand when Korean managers implicitly and indirectly delegate work. Try to remember the communication characteristics we learned in Chapter 5. Koreans tend to communicate implicitly or indirectly without verbal expression, so occasionally instructions from higher authorities may not be passed down to subordinates correctly. This may lead to insufficient information or instructions and ultimately may cause delay or misdirection in completing the delegated task. Therefore, it is important to confirm information and instructions by asking specific questions when you do not clearly understand a task delegated by a Korean manager. Many Korean managers try to avoid redoing the task from lack of information when they delegate tasks. So they will provide sufficient information when they first delegate, and continuously monitor the status and follow up with the process.

Interestingly, Koreans often delegate tasks not by job specialties, but rather by personal relationships. This is why employees who perform well or are familiar with a task will continue to be delegated more tasks. In this case, foreigners may wonder, "why is that person working on that task when it is not his/her specialty?" In contrast, some may find it upsetting if a task within his or her specialties is delegated to another employee and seriously disrupt the workflow. All this happens because Korean organizations are relationship-centered. The degree of delegation depends on each company's culture. Most managers and staff think that final decisions should be made by managers and consequently, tasks are not fully delegated to subordinates.

Case Study

Delegation 1

Anna works at a Korean company in Czech Republic. A new Korean manager has been appointed to Anna's department. When he first came to the team, he wanted to change the way things were done in his new department. Before he was appointed a manager in Anna's department he had noticed that the department entrusted a nominal amount of work to the employees while the managers were always busy with heavy workload. The new Korean manager thought that the former manager did not delegate tasks to his employees properly. On his first day at his new department in Czech Republic, he began delegating work to the employees, giving them decision-making authorities. However, Anna and her fellow employees could not understand why they were assigned these tasks and started to complain that they could not complete the delegated tasks since they had no such experience. They also complained that their wages remained same although their workload increased. Anna and her colleagues continuously asked the new Korean manager about their delegated tasks and he was kept busy answering all their questions. Eventually, the new manager's endeavor resulted in a huge mess. What could have been the problem?

Expert Opinion Anna and the rest of the employees had never been delegated these tasks. In addition, they were not prepared or trained for such delegation. Of course, they were not happy about the responsibilities that came with the delegation either. Ultimately, as we learned in Chapter 6, delegation cannot be a useful motivator if employees are not ready to accept it. The new manager should have trained them before delegating authority.

Delegation is an interaction between the one who delegates tasks and the one who is delegated with tasks. The person who delegates authority should define the scope of the delegation with reasonable expectations. On the other hand, those that are delegated with tasks should be able to understand what is expected of them.

In this case, the new manager did not consider whether the employees would be motivated by the delegation or whether they had the capabilities to handle the delegated work. In his attempt to change the organization in a short period of time, the manager became too ambitious and failed to understand his employees and their individual capacities in specific areas. Ultimately, his hasty delegation process did not give the employees enough time to adapt to the change and led to failure.

Delegation 2

You are Jana's manager and you recently promoted Jana to a management position. You instructed her about the main responsibilities as the new manager and you are currently meeting with her to confirm that she clearly understands everything. When asked how she is delegating tasks to her employees, Jana answered, "I delegate the majority of the work to Veronika. No one works better than Veronika. When I delegate work to her, she is perfect in terms of both completing the work and getting it done on time. I don't need to worry about it. However, other employees are not competent enough, so I cannot delegate to them." What can you advise to Jana?

Expert Opinion When delegating work to someone without verifying their capabilities, the risk of uncertainty can be mitigated by carefully deciding on the scope of the work, due date, continuous monitoring of the employee's progress and providing necessary training as needed. By now, you should be familiar with how much Koreans dislike uncertainty. This situation is unfair for Veronika because even though Jana recognizes Veronika's strengths and puts them to good use, Veronika has to work more than the other employees.

Such situations are common in Korea and will easily be perceived as you favoring Veronika. This is because in Korea, a lack of tasks is understood as a sign that you should quit your job. Therefore, delegating to a single person could deprive other employees of important performance measures like learning new tasks and developing their career. Perhaps Jana was reluctant to delegate to inexperienced employees due to the risk involved. However, she can mitigate these risks by closely monitoring the employee's process.

4

Information Sharing

Information collection, processing, and managing are important but it is also important to share it with those who need it in the organization. Most delays in decision-making or miscommunication within an organization boil down to a limited amount of shared information among employees. Lack of information sharing leads to inefficient work processes and may ultimately result in a lack of trust. Sharing information leads to efficiency and timely decision-making. Information sharing is especially important in the information age, in order to quickly adapt to changes and make quick decisions.

We learned earlier in Chapter 5 that there are many nonverbal ways to communicate in Korea. As a result, foreigners may have difficulty in clearly understanding the exact meaning of what is being said. Sometimes, unclear instructions from superiors will require subordinates to gather more information in trying to perform their tasks. For this reason, information sharing is doubly important when working with Koreans.

In traditional Korean corporations, information is shared hierarchically. However, recent technological advancements, especially the development of corporate intranets, have made it possible for employees to conveniently access and share information. Nevertheless, the level of information sharing between departments differs by company and is dependent on whether they stress cooperation or competition within the company.

In addition, information is commonly shared through informal channels in Korea. The quality of the information in joint projects between departments may vary widely depending on the type of relationships they have. Therefore, forming a dependable network within the company is crucial to becoming a successful manager. After all, merely doing one's job well is not all it takes to be recognized as a successful manager in Korea. Building good relationships with people inside and outside the organization is very important as well.

5
Task Structure

As reflected in its hierarchy-oriented culture, top-down approach is typically taken in task allocation in Korea. The duties of a manager are determined by the aims and objectives of each project. The employee's tasks are assigned in accordance to their supervisors. Managers control the overall flow of the work and manage the outcomes. They also assign tasks to lower-level positions.

Koreans willingly accept their given task structure based on the hierarchical system of their society, but this does not mean that employees cannot voice their opinions. The younger generations naturally voice their opinions and those who have good relationships with management have better opportunities in expressing their thoughts. They are more likely to express their opinions informally rather than formally.

Interestingly, Korean employees are largely unfamiliar with their own job descriptions. In Korea, job descriptions are typically kept in the company's personnel files for records purposes. Korean employees often perform more functions than what is stated in their job descriptions and complete tasks that are assigned in accordance to the situation. Multinational companies tend to have more detailed job descriptions though it varies by each company's culture. However, in Western countries, employees are hired to match the job descriptions, and tasks are assigned based on the specific descriptions. These cultural differences sometimes lead to conflict when Korean managers working with foreigners in local subsidiaries give tasks that are not in their job description.

Case Study

Task Structure

Jana works in the accounting department of a Korean company in Czech Republic. According to her job description, Jana's task is to close an account, draw up consolidated financial statements, and reconcile taxes. However, Jana's company will participate in a local product exhibition and the additional work associated with the exhibition is shared among the employees in the Czech office. Participation in the exhibition means creating brochures and posters, making booth reservations, planning how to display products, deciding the guide and so on, which amounts to a lot of additional work.

A task force team (TFT) was thus formed, and the head of the TFT began assigning tasks to employees regardless of their job descriptions. Jana, who is in the accounting team, is now in charge of administrative work such as making booth reservations, contacting the administrators of the exhibition and inviting guests. Jana could not understand why she had to work on these administrative tasks when her job is in accounting. So Jana asked her manager why she had to work on tasks that were not stated in her job description. If you were Jana, what would you do? If you were Jana's Korean manager, how would you explain this to Jana?

Expert Opinion By now, you are familiar with the Korean attitude toward job descriptions, which we discussed in earlier cases. In this situation, Jana's complaint and request for an explanation may be reasonable in Western culture where people work according to their job description.

However, unlike Westerners, Koreans do not work according to the job description but are allocated tasks depending on the situation. Moreover, if there is a special event in the company, everyone shares the workload regardless of the job description. Whether they are the team in charge of the special event or even when there is no one specific person in charge, everyone naturally provides support.

Special events like the said exhibition are important corporate events and do not occur often. Of course, such change in workload is often not received well in Western cultures. In Korean corporate culture, for such important one-time events for the entire company, it is implicitly understood that everyone should participate by each taking a responsibility. As we saw in Chapter 3, Koreans expand the concept of family to the scale of the organization or even to the nation in face of a large, unusual event. Koreans believe that when the entire company unites with one goal, members of the organization display greater energy.

Therefore, managers in this case should explain this to the team members and seek their understanding so that they accept their newly assigned tasks positively and proactively. Actively participating in corporate events is understood as a way of showing loyalty to one's organization in Korea. It puts an employee's work ethic in a positive light and may even affect his or her performance evaluation. This may seem irrational in a country where tasks are assigned based on job description. In that case, it would be advisable to take into account these cultural differences and come to a mutual understanding and agreement before work is assigned.

6
Teamwork

Many organizational models have been developed to reflect the organizational structure of a modern organization. Of these, the most representative model among them is the team unit. Most tasks in Korean corporations are performed in teams. While finance or sales related tasks do not require teams very much, other tasks like technology development and marketing are performed in teams or in task force units. Koreans try to promote a cooperative team atmosphere and do their best not to cause distress to the entire team by performing their best while completing the assigned tasks.

Teams in Korean corporations are unique in the sense that it is not limited to the autonomously operating teams of foreign corporations. First, let us take a look at the most typical type of team. The team system in general consists of project teams and task force teams, which overcomes the limitations of the functionally divided organization and transcends hierarchical chains of command. These teams are composed of core talent from each department to reach specific goals while retaining affiliation with their original department. While task force teams are temporarily formed to reach a specific set of goals, project teams are typically formed for long-term ongoing tasks.

In addition to autonomous work team that handles daily business operations by autonomously making decisions, cross-functional team joins specialists of different functions to collaborate on special tasks. Rather than focusing on the autonomous work teams that are common in the West, Korean companies tend to merge departments with similar tasks that interact closely to break down the hierarchy and form a flatter and slimmer organizational structure.

Koreans believe that teamwork is a driving force for better performance. This requires clear roles and responsibilities. In addition, sharing the vision and goals of the organization helps the team members to fully use their capabilities. However overly emphasizing task allocation and goal achievement can decrease the entire team's motivation. Most tasks are assigned by the team leaders and once tasks are given they are not usually adjusted between team members. Team leaders generally coordinate the members' tasks and take full responsibility for the project.

Then how are team members compensated for their performances? Performance-based compensation differs by company. Some companies compensate with team bonuses and others will offer individual rewards or reward only the highest performing members. Meanwhile, there are companies that only reward teams with recognition and without financial rewards. In such cases, employees tend to not engage actively in common tasks. The most common form of compensation for team performance in Korea is a monetary reward for the team's *hoesik*.

Case Study

Teams & Teamwork

Let us assume that you are the manager of your respective company. Your company is operating a joint project with a Korean company. A TFT has been formed for this joint project and both your company and the Korean company are working in teams. Unexpectedly, your mutual client has requested a proposal within a week. Both your company and the Korean counterpart know that this proposal cannot be completed within the normal working hours. Your Korean partner insists that they must finish the proposal either by working overtime or by adding additional members to the TFT in both companies. If you were the manager of your company, how would you handle this situation?

Expert Opinion Koreans work overtime naturally when there is an urgent and important task. When a task is given to a team, they tend to work harder in order to avoid harming the team's progress in meeting the common goal. However, working overtime for urgent tasks may not be taken for granted in other cultures that employees may get upset. That is not to say that employees of other cultures do not exert as much time and energy on urgent projects. Meeting deadlines is of utmost importance for all companies and most will do anything within their means to honor the agreement for the joint project.

Korean corporations have a very high priority in honoring an agreement and accommodating the clients' needs. This is rooted in the Korean tradition of honor and saving face. Koreans would rather work long hours at the expense of losing their personal time than not be able to meet their client's request and lose face. This is especially more so in joint projects and they often will go above and beyond to ensure that they pull their weight. Failure to meet the deadline would mean they would lose face to their client and partner, which is to be avoided at all costs. Other cultures value satisfying the clients' needs perhaps in different ways.

In Korea, if a team's work does not go smoothly or if a coworker is overwhelmed with too much work, others will try to help even if it is not part of their own task. Also, they do not feel animosity when instructed by their supervisors to share their coworker's tasks. For those that are in the same team, the common membership to the team tends to make them think that even individual tasks are common tasks. You may find that our discussion of Koreans' behavior in small groups is applicable in this situation as well.

Westerners may find this difficult to understand. However, Koreans believe that there is compensation in the long run if they contribute to a colleague's work or to the entire team. Those who contribute to the organization will establish good relationships within the organization, which will positively affect their overall performance review in Korea where performance is appraised in a multifaceted way.

However, the same small-group tendencies may result in extreme competition between teams when conflicts arise. Such cases may result in communication issues and affect overall organizational performance and should be managed carefully.

7 Timelines

Although Koreans are typically generous about time, punctuality is considered very important in business to complete tasks in a timely manner. However, their work process shows that rather than distributing work evenly throughout the allotted time, they tend to rush into work as the deadline approaches. For emergency cases from the executive management, they will work all night to meet the deadline. At times the quality of the work may suffer as they try to meet a deadline. In such cases, if quality is considered more important, they may ask for an extension to complete the work.

Deadlines set by Korean managers are often very tight. Sometimes they are so tight that it is impossible to meet the deadline. What is more amazing is that Koreans will meet these impossible deadlines! This is more so in hierarchical organizations. When Korea was trying to catch up with the developed countries in the 1960s, they focused on achieving high performance and believed that anything was possible. During this time period, Koreans were recognized in the global market for their fast construction, so they were able to obtain many contracts in foreign markets. These experiences stimulated Koreans to create a hard-working, fast-paced work environment and led to their belief that "speed" is crucial in work. However, such work ethic demanded sacrifice in personal life. Today, Koreans try to set realistic deadlines by placing a greater emphasis on the quality of work completed.

Next, let us take a quick look at overtime. Overtime payments made in the wage system have become less common as companies increasingly shift toward salary system. Rather, exceptional performance is compensated with a bonus. Generally, in countries where people highly value their time, employees will not appreciate overtime work even when appropriately compensated. However, in countries where financial compensation is highly valued, employees will willingly accept overtime work if they are compensated. In the past, there was a shortage of human resources relative to workloads in Korean organizations and employees welcomed working overtime because of the extra compensation. However, Koreans today do not appreciate overtime work although they still consider it to be part of being loyal to the company.

Case Study

Meeting a Deadline

Peter is working at a Korean company in Romania. Peter's team holds a meeting every Friday morning to review the week's work and plan for the coming week. The staff members have an opportunity to check each other's work progress and their own schedules. The third-quarter budget is Anna's responsibility and the deadline for the budget was today. In last Friday's meeting Anna did not mention anything about her work schedule. Today when Peter asked Anna for the written report, Anna replied that she still had not completed the budget. Peter was supposed to report on the budget to the headquarters, but after taking a look at Anna's work, he realized that she had not even completed 50 percent of the work and became very angry. In this situation, what should Peter do to prevent such problems from happening in the future?

Expert Opinion Peter thought that since Anna did not raise any concerns during the team meeting, the deadline would be met. Furthermore, Peter was even more upset since he was supposed to have a conference call regarding Anna's results with the headquarters in Korea. He was worried that Koreans would not understand this situation.

Koreans consider it very important to adhere to deadlines. As mentioned in Chapter 1, you may remember that impatient Koreans sometimes say "*bbali-bbali*" (hurry-hurry). This is especially more so in hierarchical cultures where the ability to meet deadlines set by one's boss is considered very important. However, deadlines are always understood as firm in Korea.

Peter needs to emphasize the importance of meeting deadlines at staff meetings. This is something that needs to be done regardless of the culture. If you cannot meet a deadline, it is important to notify others in advance. In addition, Peter should continue to follow-up until this becomes the norm in the work process. Also, if employees need his support to proceed with a task, he needs to address them as the manager.

8 Planning

Korea's conglomerates have specific departments for planning where their long-term strategies are established. The long-term strategies of multinational companies usually come from their overseas headquarters or regional headquarters, so they focus on short-term planning internally. In owner-operated businesses, long-term planning is common while short-term planning is more common in public corporations where CEOs change often.

In organizations where planning is not central, plans are not strict guidelines but rather frameworks for the business operation. Koreans sometimes use plans as a tool for performance measurement rather than as a strict guideline for productivity. In addition, planning is usually the responsibility of managers or higher-level executives.

9 Conflict Management

Because it is more efficient to work together with others rather than working alone, organizations are formed. By becoming a member of the organization and achieving the organizational goal, we also achieve our personal goals. While it seems obvious that organizational members that share a common goal should be cooperative with each other, it is not always so.

A successful organization requires maintaining good human relationships and interactions. How two or more people come together to share work and complete tasks define a successful organization. However, even when the members know that they should cooperate to achieve a common goal, they sometimes have different personal objectives, compete with each other, and create conflicts or compromise with each other. The degrees of conflict and cooperation among members strongly influence the organizational operation and effectiveness. More importantly, it should be noted that depending on the situation, conflicts can sometimes help the organization. That is why it is necessary to be able to resolve conflict and negotiate to achieve the common organizational goal.

So let us see how Koreans resolve conflicts that occur within an organization. Koreans generally do not like conflict. Conflict has a strong, negative connotation in hierarchical and collectivistic cultures and creates a situation where one could lose face. Thus, in a culture that avoids and prevents conflict, people stress harmony, especially in relationships. As we learned in Chapter 5, Koreans generally have an indirect and circumvent communication style that is rooted in their efforts not to publicly show conflict. Also, because job mobility is very low in Korea, maintaining good relationships with one's colleagues is crucial since one cannot readily leave his or her jobs in the face of conflict.

When conflicts arise, Koreans will not attempt to directly and openly resolve conflicts but will resolve them informally over meals or tea. Perhaps this would be most commonly done over drinks after work. Sometimes mediators, usually managers, are elected to resolve problems between coworkers. In severe cases, conflict can escalate into a public outburst of emotions. Even in such cases, it is strange to see how they are easily resolved after having dinner or drinks together. Perhaps they are only pretending to be okay? We will never know but this ultimately facilitates smooth operations within the organization. Once a conflict is resolved, Koreans try not to hold grudges because holding grudges means that they have not completely kept their agreement of reconciliation. To break such agreement would mean losing face.

If you are in a conflict with a Korean, do not try to resolve it immediately. Trying to resolve the conflict in due time, preferably in an informal get together over drinks or with mediators, would prove to be much easier than you think. One resolves hard feelings over a dinner or drinks in Korea. Once a conflict is resolved between Korean men, they often become much closer friends.

10
Organizational Structure

What is organizational structure? Let us use an example. In order to build a generator, there needs to be links between processes, between workers, between human and material resources for the processes, and between all of these entities for thousands of parts to be assembled in the right order. The links between the members of the organization is called the organizational structure.

Corporations typically grow from a unit to a functional structure and a multi-functional structure as they diversify. However, Korean organizations tend to diversify by forming corporate groups rather than forming a multi-business organization. Therefore, while Western corporations have many businesses within a single organization, each business becomes a subsidiary within a corporate group in Korea. In multi-business organizations of the West, each business generally operates autonomously under decentralized management, while in Korea, each subsidiary operates under the control of the secretary of the president or a supervising department. Each corporate group has different levels of control. While in the past the subsidiaries were strictly controlled at the corporate group level, in recent years, autonomous management of subsidiaries has been encouraged.

Regardless of organizational structure, decision-making is skewed toward the executive management in Korean companies. Positions are professionalized, specified and layered, and business operations tend to be highly formalized and documented. This indicates that the organizational structures of Korean corporations are largely bureaucratic and centralized. The organizational structure is more vertical than horizontal. The formalization, centralization, and vertical stratification of organizational structure in Korean companies have a lot to do with the patriarchal family system and the hierarchical nature of Korean culture.

Korea's conglomerates are also called *jaebeol*. Each *jaebeol* was mainly composed of family members and relatives. They rose during the 1960s as a result of the Korean government's political and economic demands. Park Chung-hee, the president of Korea at the time, expected *jaebeol* to fulfill their role as the drivers of economic development and supported them with cheap capital with his political influence. Under this policy, *jaebeol* grew to account for 50 percent of Korea's GDP and export in the mid-1990s. However, the financial crisis of 1997 and the IMF intervention stifled Korea's economic growth. It was then understood that the *jaebeol* structure was not up to the global standards and led to the weakening of this system.

Korea's large organizations are considered very centralized and formal. Without Confucian tradition and loyalty from their members, it would be impossible to maintain such large organizations in a centralized and formalized structure.

Summary of Chapter 7

1. Employment

- Today's Korean corporations prefer challenging and creative talent. They dedicate a significant amount of time to recruit these talents during interviews.

2. Decision-Making

- Korea's hierarchical culture leads to top-down decision-making.
- Decisions in an organization are generally made by those at or above managerial positions. Most critical decisions are made by the executive management.

3. Delegation

- Traditionally, Korean companies have had difficulty with delegation, resulting in a military-like organizations. This organizational form proved to be inefficient, so today's corporations are strongly encouraging delegation.
- Managers want to share detailed tasks with their subordinates and delegation is often used as a means of empowerment and motivation.

4. Information Sharing

- Information is commonly shared through informal channels in Korea. The quality of the information in joint projects between departments may vary widely depending on the type of relationships they have.

5. Task Structure

- Koreans generally take on more responsibilities than is written in their job description and rather than following the job description, they work on tasks as they arise in a given situation.

6. Teamwork

- Koreans believe that teamwork is a driving force for better performance.
- Clear roles and responsibilities are required for effective teamwork. Sharing the vision and goals of the organization also helps the team members to fully utilize their capabilities.

7. Timelines

- Although Koreans are typically generous about time, punctuality is considered very important in business and deadlines for tasks are strictly observed.

8. Planning

- Korea's conglomerates have specific departments for planning where their long-term strategies are established. In project-based organizations, planning is the main task, and sub-plans are established to execute the larger plan.

9. Conflict Management

- Koreans generally do not like conflict. Conflict has a strong, negative connotation in hierarchical and collectivistic cultures and creates a situation where one could lose face. Koreans will not attempt to directly and openly resolve conflict but will resolve it informally over meals or tea. Perhaps it would be most commonly done over drinks after work.

10. Organizational Structure

- Regardless of organizational structure, decision-making is skewed toward the executive management in Korean companies. Positions are professionalized, specified, and layered. Business operations tend to be highly formalized and documented.

Notes

Chapter 1

1 "Worldwide No.1 Fields of South Korea," *Hankook Ilbo*, November 22, 2011. www.koreatimes.com/article/697437

2 *Statistics Collections of Korea in the World* (Seoul: The Korea International Trade Association, Institute for International Trade, 2011).

3 *Population Survey* (Seoul: Statistics Korea, 2010).

4 Ibid.

5 Ibid.

6 From the Seoul Metropolitan Government. www.seoul.go.kr/v2007/seoul/review/general/mean_brandseoul.html

7 From the Korea Meteorological Administration. www.kma.go.kr

8 From the website www.yonhapnews.co.kr/economy/2010/12/17/0301000000AKR20101217157900002.HTML

9 *Population Aging in the World and Korea* (Seoul: Statistics Korea, 2009).

10 Kim Gi-cheon, "The Origin of Korean," *Chosun Ilbo*, December 11, 2009. http://news.chosun.com/site/data/html_dir/2009/12/11/2009121101577.html

11 Hwang Gye-sik, "The Economic Strength of South Korea Is 19 Times that of North Korea," *Segye Ilbo*, November 4, 2011. www.segye.com/Articles/News/Politics/Article.asp?aid=20120117004806&subctg1=&subctg2=

12 Park Woo-hee, *The Economic Development of Korea* (Cheonan: Independence Hall, Institute for the History of Korean Independence Movement, 1989), p. 27.

13 Park Woo-hee, *The Economic Development of Korea* (Cheonan: Independence Hall, Institute for the History of Korean Independence Movement, 1989), pp. 42-43.

14 *Economically Active Population List per Year* (Gyeongido: Ministry of Strategy and Finance).

15 Ibid.

16 Choi Jong-go, *The History of the Diplomatic Interactions between Korea and Germany* (Seoul: Hongsungsa, 1983), pp. 300-302.

17 Ibid.

18 Park Woo-hee, *The Economic Development of Korea* (Cheonan: Independence Hall, Institute for the History of Korean Independence Movement, 1989), p. 83.

Chapter 2

1 Diagram adapted from A. Norenzayan, E. E. Smith, B. J. Kim, and R. E. Nisbett, "Cultural Preferences for Formal versus Intuitive Reasoning", *Cognitive Science*, vol. 26, Issue 5 (Texas: Cognitive Science Society, 2002), p. 664.

2 A. Norenzayan, E. E. Smith, B. J. Kim, and R. E. Nisbett, "Cultural Preferences for Formal versus Intuitive Reasoning", *Cognitive Science*, vol. 26, Issue 5 (Texas: Cognitive Science Society, 2002), pp. 653-684.

3 S. Kitayama and H. R. Markus, "Culture and Self: How Cultures Influence the Way We View Ourselves", *People: Psychology from a Cultural Perspective* (California: Thomson Books/Cole Publishing Co., 1994), pp. 17-37.

4 D. Cohen, E. Hoshino-Browne, and A. K. Leung, "Culture and Structure of Personal Experience: Insider and Outsider Phenomenologies of the Self and Social World", *Advances in Experimental Social Psychology* vol. 39 (California: Academic Press, 2007), pp. 1-67.

5 M. W. Morris and K. Peng, "Culture and Cause: American and Chinese Attributions for Social and Physical Events", *Journal of Personality and Social Psychology* vol. 67 (Washington, D.C.: American Psychological Association, 1994), pp. 949-971.

6 Ibid.

7 Edward Hall, *Beyond Culture* (New York: Anchor Books, 1977), pp. 90-94.

8 M. Imai and D. Gentner, "A Cross-Linguistic Study of Early Word Meaning: Universal Ontology and Linguistic Influence", *Cognition* vol. 62, Issue 2 (Massachusetts: Elsevier Inc., 1997), pp. 62, 169-200.

9 L.-J. Ji, Z. Zhang, and R. E. Nisbett, "Is It Culture or Is It Language? Examination of Language Effects in Cross-Cultural Research on Categorization", *Journal of Personality and Social Psychology*, vol. 87(1) (Washington, D.C.: American Psychological Association, 2004), pp. 57-65.

10 T. Masuda, R. Gonzalez, L. Kwan, and R. E. Nisbett, "Culture and Aesthetic Preference: Comparing the Attention to Context of East Asians and Americans", *Personality and Social Psychology Bulletin* (California: SAGE Publications, 2008), pp. 1260-1275.

11 Ruth Benedict, *The Chrysanthemum and the Sword: Patterns of Japanese Culture* (New York: New American Library, 1946), pp. 2-3.

12 *Population Changes by Religion Type* (Seoul: Statistics Korea, 2005).

Other References

1 Richard Nisbett, *The Geography of Thought* (New York: Free Press, 2003).

2 EBS and Kim Myeong-jin, *East and West* (Gyeongido: Wisdom house, 2009).

3 Northcote Parkinson, *East and West* (Boston: Houghton Mifflin, 1963).

4 Luce Irigaray, *Entre Orient et Occident* (Paris: Editions Grasset et Fasquelle, 1999).

5 Herman Dooyeweerd, *Roots of Western Culture* (New York: Edwin Mellen Pr., 2003).

6 Kim Yong-un, *Japanese and Korean: Or the Sword and the Brush* (Seoul: The Deep Rooted Tree, 1981).

Chapter 3

1 *Social Indicator of Korea* (Seoul: Statistics Korea, 2010).

2 *Ethnologue* (Texas: SIL International, 2009).

3 MBC Documentary 'The Power of Hangul' (Seoul: MBC, 2008).

Chapter 6

1 Hong Ji-in, "76.8 Percent of Workers Considered Quitting or Changing Their Job Due to Their Supervisor," *Hankook Ilbo*, November, 27, 2009. http://news.hankooki.com/lpage/society/200911/h2009112710300021950.htm